LOVE UNVEILED

EDWARD SRI

LOVE UNVEILED

The Catholic Faith Explained

IGNATIUS PRESS   SAN FRANCISCO

Cover art:
Crucifixion with the Virgin Mary and Saint John
Mosaic in the apse, early 12th century
San Clemente Basilica, Rome
© Alfredo Dagli Orti/The Art Archive at Art Resource, New York

Cover design by Devin Schadt, Saint Louis Creative

© 2015 by Edward Sri
Published 2015 by Ignatius Press, San Francisco
All rights reserved
ISBN 978-1-62164-028-8
Library of Congress Control Number 2015930778
Printed in the United States of America ∞

With gratitude to three teachers who are also witnesses:

Scott Hahn
Barbara Morgan
Fr. Paul Murray, O.P.

CONTENTS

ACKNOWLEDGMENTS

This book is based on the Augustine Institute's twenty-part documentary video series, *Symbolon: The Catholic Faith Explained*, of which I served as the host and content director. It was a tremendous blessing to work over the course of two and a half years with a team of amazing presenters, writers, videographers, theologians, and catechetical experts in the planning, writing, filming, and editing of the program. The hard work and insights that many people brought to the video series have no doubt contributed to this book.

I first thank Augustine Institute president Tim Gray for inviting me to direct the *Symbolon* program. It was his commitment to the New Evangelization and his vision for the Institute's parish faith-formation programs that made the *Symbolon* series possible. I also am grateful to Sean Innerst for his original concepts for *Symbolon*, his foundational curriculum outline for the video series, and his continued valuable contribution into the development of the program.

I also thank the Institute's video production team, most especially Justin Leddick, Kevin Mallory, and John Schmidt, for pouring their lives into making *Symbolon* such a beautiful and engaging series. Some of the outlines and scripts we crafted together for the videos served as a basis for some of the chapters in this book. And some of the images come from their filming of the program.

Particular thanks goes to Lucas Pollice, *Symbolon* associate director. His catechetical expertise and rich pastoral experience were invaluable as we were designing the *Symbolon* series to be an easy-to-use and effective resource for adult faith formation, RCIA, and small groups. I am grateful for his wise catechetical counsel and his careful reading of the manuscript for this book.

I also acknowledge the many catechists, teachers, and diocesan leaders who gave advice and guidance in the development of the *Symbolon* program: Michael Andrews, Keith Borchers, Steve Bozza, Chris Burgwald, James Cavanaugh, Chris Chapman, Father Dennis Gill, Jim Gontis, Lisa Gulino, Mary Hanbury, Deacon Ray Helgeson, Ann Lankford, Deacon Kurt Lucas, Sean Martin, Martha Tonn, Kyle Neilson, Michelle Nilsson, Ken Ogorek, Claude Sasso, Scott Sollom, Deacon Jim Tighe, Mary Ann Weisinger, and Gloria Zapian. Their insights into the curriculum and method of the *Symbolon* video series have contributed to the approach taken in this accompanying book.

I also am grateful to Ben Akers, Christopher Blum, Mark Giszczak, Curtis Mitch, Jared Staudt, and Kyrstyn Walsh for their feedback on certain sections of the book.

Most of all, I express gratitude to my wife, Elizabeth, for her constant prayers, encouragement, and support and her helpful editorial suggestions amid the raising of our children.

INTRODUCTION

Man cannot live without love.... His life is senseless if love is not revealed to him, if he does not encounter love, if he does not experience it and make it his own, if he does not participate intimately in it.

— John Paul II, *Redemptor Hominis*[1]

If you were to walk into a coffee shop and randomly ask people, "What does the Catholic Church stand for?" what kind of responses do you think you would receive? Some people might talk about the rituals of the Catholic faith. Others might mention the pope or the Blessed Virgin Mary. A large number probably would focus on controversial moral issues of our day: "The Catholic Church is against abortion, against contraception, and against gay marriage."

Few, however, would get to the heart of the gospel and say, "The Catholic Church stands for the God who is madly in love with you, who has a plan for you and wants you to be happy—the God who even sent his Son, Jesus Christ, to die for you, who wants to forgive you and help you in your life, and who, most of all, wants an intimate, personal relationship with you so that you can be with him forever in heaven."

[1]John Paul II, Encyclical Letter *Redemptor Hominis*, March 4, 1979, no. 10, http://w2.vatican.va/content/john-paul-ii/en/encyclicals/documents/hf_jp -ii_enc_04031979_redemptor-hominis.html. All quotations from papal encyclicals are from the Vatican's website unless otherwise indicated.

Basilica of San Clemente, interior, Rome

This, quite frankly, is not the impression the average person out in the world has about the Catholic faith. And the fact of the matter is many of us who grew up Catholic don't always see our faith this way either. We might have heard there were twelve apostles, Ten Commandments, seven sacraments, and three Persons of the Trinity. But many practicing Catholics admit that they have almost zero understanding about how it all fits together and what difference it makes for their lives.

I know that was once the case in my own life.

I grew up Catholic, believed in God, showed up at Mass on Sundays, and in general wanted to be a "good person". But as I entered my adult years, many other things captured my attention more: striving for success, making money, having friends, having fun. I still went through the motions in my faith, but God was not really the priority in my life.

I also began to have a lot of questions: Is all this Catholic stuff really true? What about the other religions in the world? Does it actually matter whether I'm Catholic? And then there were all those moral issues about life, sex, and marriage: Shouldn't each individual be able to make up his own morality? Why can't we just love people and get along?

Over time, the faith started to come together for me. Thanks to God's grace and many good friends, mentors, and books, I began to sense that there was something deeper behind the various doctrines, rituals, and hierarchies of the Church. These guides helped me to appreciate more the truth and beauty of the Catholic faith and opened up for me many treasures in my faith that I had taken for granted or didn't even realize were there. Most of all, the faith began to make more sense to me—not just as a theory, but as *a whole way of life*.

This Catholic way of life that attracted me—and millions of others throughout the centuries—is ultimately the way of love: a most profound love that the world itself does not offer. But it's the love for which we are made, a love that corresponds to our hearts' deepest desires. In fact, all of our authentic forms of love—whether it be love for one's country, one's friend, one's child, or one's spouse—are meant to be drawn up into this one love that is God himself (see 1 Jn 4:8, 16). And as we will see throughout this book, it's only in this divine love that we will find our happiness and fullness of life.

Love Unveiled

Though not often appreciated in this way, the Catholic faith actually emphasizes the centrality of love more than any other religion, spirituality, or philosophy in the world.

Grotto of the Annunciation, Basilica of the Annunciation, Nazareth

We don't just believe in a divine power that moves the universe, but in a God who, in his very essence, *is* love—indeed, a communion of love: Father, Son, and Holy Spirit. And even though this God was perfectly happy in himself, he freely chose to bring us into existence so that he could *share* his love with us.

What is even more remarkable is that this God loves with an intimate, personal love and constantly pursues a relationship with us, even when we have turned away from him in sin. He still hungers for our attention. He thirsts for our love. The Bible describes our God as a good shepherd seeking his lost sheep, a woman searching for her lost coin, a father ardently running out to meet his lost son. As one recent pope said, God is not just Creator and Lord, but also "a lover with all the passion of a true love".[2] So intense is God's love for us that it's as if he could not bear to remain separated from us. His love drove him to become one of us in Jesus Christ, and it drove him to offer his life for our sins so that we could be one with him again.

On the cross, Jesus reveals most fully not only the total self-giving love of our God, but also the great love to which we are all called. On the night before he died, in fact, Jesus commanded his disciples, "[L]ove one another as I have loved you" (Jn 15:12; see Jn 13:34). The way he loves—totally, freely, sacrificially, and unconditionally—is now the standard for our lives. Indeed, this is how God made us, and we will find our happiness only in living like Christ, in self-giving love.

This, however, is not just some external command imposed on us from the outside, a high ethical bar over which we have to leap in order to please God and get to heaven. Left to our own powers, we could never love as God has loved us. But Catholic Christianity emphasizes that God actually invites us to *participate in his divine love*. Here, we come to what is arguably the most astonishing aspect of the Catholic faith. God doesn't just pardon us of our sins. He wants to fill us with his life. He wants to transform our hearts. He seeks to heal, perfect, and even elevate our human love, so that it participates in his own perfect, divine love. This is what God has been doing throughout the centuries in the lives of countless ordinary Christians: changing our minds and hearts, so that we can begin to see as he sees, and love as he loves. Through God's grace—his very divine life in us—we can begin to love in a much more profound way than we ever could on our own, for, as Saint

[2]Benedict XVI, *Deus Caritas Est*, December 25, 2005, no. 10.

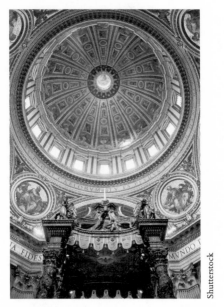

St. Peter's Basilica, interior, Vatican City

Paul once wrote, "[I]t is no longer I who live, but Christ who lives in me" (Gal 2:20).[3]

Encountering Christ: The Head and the Heart

In this book, we will see how everything about the Catholic faith leads us further on a lifelong journey of growing in the love of God. Through his Spirit dwelling in us, God

---

[3] As Saint Thérèse of Lisieux once said to God of her fellow religious sisters in the convent, "Never would I be able to love my Sisters as You love them, unless *You*, O my Jesus, *loved them in me*" (St. Thérèse of Lisieux, *Story of a Soul* [Washington: ICS Publications, 1976], 221; emphasis in original).

draws us ever more out of ourselves—out of our fears, our limited perspectives, our selfishness, our pursuits for our own pleasure, comfort, and gain—and toward him and toward our neighbor in love. Through the Church, the communion of saints, and especially through the sacraments, we don't just receive God's love; "we enter into the very dynamic of his self-giving."[4]

In this book, we will walk through the "big picture" of the Catholic faith, from creation, the Cross, and the Church, to the sacraments, Catholic social teaching, and sexual ethics, to purgatory, the papacy, and prayer. In the process, we will see how all the various aspects of the faith fit together into the one overarching story of God's love and our being caught up in that love. And we will use the *Catechism of the Catholic Church* for our itinerary. The *Catechism*, the official summary of Catholic teaching for our day, has four main pillars: the Creed, the sacraments, moral life, and prayer. The Creed is the summary of the story of God's love: his plan of salvation from creation to Christ to the Last Judgment. The sacraments are how God draws us into this story of his love by filling us with his life. The moral life is our response to God's love in the way we live. And prayer is our response to God's love in our interior life.

Our understanding of the faith and our ability to live it out, however, is not something that is formed in a vacuum. We live in a certain cultural setting that influences our hearts and minds. The increasingly secular, relativistic, and individualistic attitudes around us can affect the way we think about God, life, love, and happiness. So as we walk through core Catholic beliefs, we will address common questions people in our culture have, such as the following:

---

[4] Benedict XVI, *Deus Caritas Est*, no. 13.

- Why do I need the Church? Can't I just be spiritual on my own?
- Isn't one religion just as good as another?
- How is the death of a man two thousand years ago, in a city far away, relevant for my life today?
- Why does the Church talk about morality so much? Can't I make up my own morality? And besides, shouldn't we stop imposing our views on other people?
- Is it really our responsibility to care for the poor? Doesn't God help those who help themselves?
- Along the way, we'll also address questions some of our Protestant brothers and sisters have regarding topics such as Mary, the Bible, confession, the papacy, and the Mass.

But our walk through the Catholic faith will be much more than an intellectual enterprise. We will learn spiritual lessons from the beauty of the Catholic tradition and the insights of the saints. And we will be encouraged constantly to make application to our daily lives, considering how the various aspects of the faith invite us to a deeper conversion—to love God more and entrust more of our lives to him. This book, thus, aims to form not just the head, but also the heart. My hope is that this book not only helps you understand Jesus and his plan of salvation, but inspires you to love him more. For this is what the faith is all about: "Being Christian is not the result of an ethical choice or a lofty idea, but the encounter with an event, a person, which gives life a new horizon and a decisive direction."[5]

---

[5] Ibid., no. 1.

Chapter One

The God Who Is Love

One of the most profound statements ever written about God is found in the biblical text known as the First Letter of John. The statement consists of just three simple words: "God is love" (1 Jn 4:8, 16).

This verse gets to the heart of the distinctively Christian understanding of God. While the vast majority of people in the world believe there is a God, many do not really believe in a *personal* God—a God who loves us, who reveals himself to us, and who calls us to an intimate relationship with him. Rather, some view God as a vague higher power like "the force" in the movie *Star Wars*. Others believe in a God, but not one who really interacts in this world and is involved in our daily lives. Some think of God as a harsh judge. Still others make God in their own image, assuming God supports whatever ideas, choices, and lifestyles they may have and never challenges them to change.

But the Bible offers a very different picture of God: "God is love". And in this opening chapter, we will take a closer look at what this means. We will see that God himself exists as a profound communion of love, a Trinity, and that he created us out of love and invites us into an intimate personal relationship of love. The God who *is* love created us *out of* love, and made us *for* his love.

Basilica of St. Praxedes, detail, Rome

The Holy Trinity

When Saint John states, "God is love", he is not simply describing a quality of God (God is loving) or saying that love is something God possesses (God has a lot of love) or merely affirming that loving is something God does (God loves). Rather, Saint John is underscoring how love is at the very essence of who God is: God *is* love. And in the words of theologian Father Robert Barron, "This means that God must be, in his own life, an interplay of lover (the Father), beloved (the Son) and shared love (the Holy Spirit)."[1]

This sheds light on the Christian doctrine of the Trinity—the belief that there is one God who exists as three divine

---

[1] Robert Barron, *Catholicism* (New York: Image Books, 2011), 85.

Persons: Father, Son, and Holy Spirit. It is this triune God that Jesus Christ fully revealed some two thousand years ago—a God who, in his very essence, is love.

As a faithful Jew, Jesus affirmed the traditional Jewish conviction of monotheism, belief in only one God (see Mk 12:29–30). But he also revealed something new about the inner life of the one true God.

First, Jesus gave a deeper understanding of God as Father. Previously, the Jewish people had invoked God as Father in the sense that God was the Creator of the world, the Giver of the law, and the One who guided and protected his people. Jesus, however, revealed God as Father in a totally new way. Long before God created the universe and established his relationship with Israel, the Father existed as a Father in relation to his Son.[2] And what is most remarkable is that Jesus identifies himself as that eternal Son of the Father. He spoke of himself as the beloved Son who was sent by God the Father (see Jn 3:16). At the same time, while he is distinct from the Father, Jesus also spoke and acted as God himself. Indeed, Jesus, who affirmed belief in only one God, saw himself on par with God the Father, so much so that he could say, "I and the Father are one" (Jn 10:30).

Second, at the Last Supper Jesus promised to send another advocate, the Holy Spirit, to be with and in the disciples. He describes the Spirit also as having divine qualities, proceeding from the Father and the Son, guiding the disciples "into all the truth" (Jn 16:13; see Jn 14:17, 26), and taking what the Son possesses and giving it to his disciples (see Jn 16:15). Jesus thus reveals the Spirit as a divine Person along with himself and the Father.

---

[2] "He is eternally Father in relation to his only Son" (*Catechism of the Catholic Church*, 2nd ed. [Washington, D.C.: Libreria Editrice Vaticana—United States Catholic Conference, 2000], no. 240; hereafter cited as *CCC*).

Love Unveiled

The most famous reference Jesus made to the three Persons of the Trinity came after his Resurrection when he commissioned his apostles to baptize all nations "in the name of the Father and of the Son and of the Holy Spirit" (Mt 28:19). The early Christians expressed this trinitarian faith in their own worship of God in the ritual of the sacrament of baptism, in the statements of faith known as the Creed, and in the eucharistic liturgy, which echoes the praise found at the end of Paul's letters: "The grace of the Lord Jesus Christ and the love of God and the fellowship of the Holy Spirit be with you all" (2 Cor 13:14; cf. 1 Cor 12:4–6; Eph 4:4–6).

Daring to Approach the Mystery

But how can this be? How can there be three Persons but only one God? This is a great mystery, indeed the central mystery of the faith, for it is the mystery of God himself. Our small, finite minds cannot fully grasp the essence of the infinite, all-powerful, all-good, all-loving God. We will spend all eternity contemplating the mystery of the triune God.

Mankind wouldn't dare to contemplate the hidden life of God unless Jesus himself had revealed it. And although the full mystery is beyond the grasp of our limited human reason, we can know something about God's inner life and at least *begin* to appreciate how it makes sense that God exists as Trinity.

All creation bears the mark of the Creator to some degree. Saint Augustine said there are "traces" of the Trinity throughout creation, and various analogies have been used throughout the centuries to express the mystery of the three Persons in one God.[3] Some have used the example of fire, which has flame, heat, and light. Others have turned to the shamrock,

---

[3] St. Augustine, *On the Trinity*, book XV, chap. 2.

From the *Symbolon* series

Baptism of Christ by Maratta (copy in St. Peter's Basilica, Vatican City)

the one clover with three leaves. Augustine himself focused on the individual person, the one creature God specifically made in his own "image" and "likeness" (Gen 1:26). In one of his analogies,[4] Augustine noted that when a person has a proper, healthy love for himself, there are three dynamics at work: the person's mind must first have a thought, an understanding of himself, and when he is aware of himself, he can love himself.[5] Augustine sees in this personal three-fold dynamic between one's mind, one's self-understanding,

---

[4] Ibid., book IX, chap. 3ff.

[5] We know from our own experience that we can have moments of introspection when we come to a deeper understanding of ourselves—why we do what we do, why we react the way we react, what our hearts' deeper desires are. This may happen on a business trip, vacation, or retreat, when we're away from our daily routines and have more time to reflect. Or it may happen in a good conversation about our lives with a close friend, a priest, or a counselor. And with that greater self-understanding often comes a deeper level of love and self-acceptance.

and one's love—all within the human being—a reflection of
the Trinity. If God loves himself, he must have an understanding of himself. There must be a lover (the Father) and
a beloved (the Son). And there must also be the shared
love itself (the Holy Spirit) between the lover and beloved.
"When Father and Son gaze at each other, they breathe back
and forth their mutual love, and this is the *amor sui* [self-love]
of God, or the Holy Spirit. Hence we have three dynamisms
but not three Gods; we have a lover, a beloved, and a shared
love, within the unity of one substance, not a one plus one
plus one adding up to three, but a one times one times one,
equaling one."[6]

To Know and to Love

Another helpful approach is to consider how man has the
ability to know and to love, two powers that reflect God himself, who is all-knowing and all-loving. Let's take a moment
to ponder what God's being all-knowing and all-loving might
tell us about the Trinity.

First, if God is all-knowing, he knows everything perfectly. He knows even himself perfectly. Now think about
what that would mean. Right now, you as a person can close
your eyes and have a thought of yourself, an image of yourself in your mind. But that idea of yourself remains just that,
an idea in your head. You wouldn't say that the thought you
have of yourself is another person.

With God, however, it's different. If God knows everything perfectly, and he knows even himself perfectly, then
his thought of himself has to be a perfect mirror image of
himself. All that is in him must be in the idea of himself

[6]Barron, *Catholicism*, 87.

or he wouldn't know himself perfectly. As one Catholic writer explained, "The idea that God has of himself cannot be imperfect. Whatever is in the Father must be in his idea of himself, and must be exactly the same as it is in himself. Otherwise God would have an inadequate idea of himself, which would be nonsense."[7] It is this very living thought of himself, this image of himself, that Christians call God the Son, the second Person of the Trinity.

But what about the third Person of the Trinity? We can proceed by considering how God is also all-loving. The Father and Son look upon each other with love. There is, thus, an infinite dialogue of love between the divine thinker and the thought, between the Father and Son. Each pours himself totally in love to the other, holding nothing back. And that infinite outpouring of love between the Father and Son is the Holy Spirit, the third Person of the Trinity. The Holy Spirit is the bond of love between the Father and the Son.

So we can see that God in his inner life is not just a Creator, a higher power, a master of the universe. In his very essence, he is a profound communion of love. The twentieth-century Christian writer C. S. Lewis once said the doctrine of the Trinity is the most important difference between Christianity and all other religions: "In Christianity God is not a static thing—not even a person—but a dynamic, pulsating activity, a life, almost a kind of drama. Almost ... a kind of dance. The union between the Father and Son is such a live concrete thing that this union itself is also a Person."[8] The Father loves the Son, and the Son in return loves the Father. Quite fittingly, the very outpouring of love between the Father and Son—the Holy Spirit—has often been called the breath or bond or kiss of love between the Father and Son.

---

[7] Frank Sheed, *Theology for Beginners* (Ann Arbor, Mich.: Servant, 1981), 34.
[8] C. S. Lewis, *Mere Christianity* (New York: Macmillan, 1960), 153.

*Father, Son, and Holy Spirit (detail in Disputation of the
Eucharist by Raphael), Vatican Museums, Vatican City*

These are just analogies, attempts to shed light on the mystery of the hidden life of God himself, not complete explanations. But the Trinity is not an abstract concept merely for scholars and theologians. We will now see how viewing God not just as "higher power" but as Father, Son, and Holy Spirit makes all the difference in the world for understanding who we are and the fullness of life to which God calls us.

Image of God

The opening scene of the Bible makes a subtle but very important point about God and our relationship with him.

In the dramatic biblical account of creation, God is described as bringing the universe into being simply by the power of his word. He says, for example, " 'Let there be light'; and there was light" (Gen 1:3). Similar language is consistently repeated when God makes the sun, moon, and stars; the land, sky, and, sea; and all the plants and animals that fill the earth. He simply gives his divine fiat: "Let there be ..."

But at the climax of the creation narrative, when God creates man and woman, he uses a strikingly different expression. God says, "Let us make man in our image, after our likeness" (Gen 1:26).

Notice how the one indivisible God suddenly starts speaking in the first person plural: "Let *us* ... in *our* image ... *our* likeness." God didn't proceed as he had in his previous acts of creation. He didn't just command, "Let there be man." He said, "Let *us* make man". Some have seen in this expression an allusion, a hint, to what Saint John Paul II called the "divine We"—the Trinity. John Paul II says it's as if God, before creating man and woman, pauses to seek "the pattern and inspiration" for his crowning work of creation. And he doesn't look outside of himself, out into the newly created universe, for his model. Rather, "the Creator as it were withdraws into himself ... in the mystery of his Being, which is already here disclosed as the divine 'We'."[9] And he creates man in the image and likeness of himself.

Living Like the Trinity

Indeed, when we read Genesis 1:26 in light of the whole of Scripture, we can see that we are made in the image and likeness, not just of some impersonal spiritual power or Supreme Being, but of the God who exists as a divine communion

---

[9]John Paul II, *Letter to Families*, February 2, 1994, no. 6.

of Persons, the Holy Trinity. And that tells us a lot about ourselves. As John Paul II taught, our bearing the image and likeness of God has an important "trinitarian character": we are made to reflect not just some vague deity we call "God", but the *triune* God.

But what does this mean? How are we to image the Trinity in the world? Man does this in a variety of ways, but one thing that stands out is our call to self-giving love. We've seen how God's very inner life is a communion of love—the love of the Father, Son, and Holy Spirit. Being made in the image and likeness of *this* God tells us that we are made for communion and self-giving. As the *Catechism* explains, "God is love and in Himself He lives a mystery of personal loving communion. Creating the human race in His own image, ... God inscribed in the humanity of man and woman the vocation, and thus the capacity and responsibility, of love and communion."[10]

This is a profound law of reality. We are made in the image and likeness of the Trinity. Written into the fabric of our being, therefore, is this law of self-giving. The Creator left his trinitarian fingerprints on us to such a degree that only in self-giving love—only when we live for God and for others—will we find the happiness we were made for. As the Catholic Church has taught, "man ... cannot fully find himself except through a sincere gift of himself".[11]

Giving or Grasping?

This stands in stark contrast with what the world says will make us happy. Instead of self-giving, many of us tend to

---

[10] *CCC* 2331, quoting John Paul II, Apostolic Exhortation *Familiaris Consortio*, November 22, 1981, no. 11.

[11] Vatican II, Pastoral Constitution on the Church in the Modern World, *Gaudium et Spes*, December 7, 1965, no. 24.

Basilica of St. John Lateran, interior, Rome

focus on what we can get out of life for ourselves. Instead of making our lives a gift to God and others, we live more for ourselves, filling ourselves up with the honors, pleasures, and things of this world. We pour our lives into our careers, driven to find our fulfillment in success, wealth, important positions, recognition, or applause. We have an urgent need to keep ourselves constantly entertained—living on screens, pursuing frivolous amusements, seeking the pleasures of food, drink, or sex—thinking that if we could just have more of these experiences, our hearts will be satisfied. It's as if we subconsciously say to ourselves, "If I could just have X—whether it be a certain job, a purchase, a boyfriend, an award—then I would finally be happy."

One great saint for our modern world is Saint Augustine, an impressive man who passionately pursued all that the world had to offer. Born in A.D. 353, Augustine achieved great success in his career as a teacher and scholar, but that was not enough. He pursued wisdom; earned positions of great honor, including a most noble teaching position in the Roman imperial court; and was financially rewarded. But still, he longed for something more. He also had the kind of social life many in the world envied: friends, parties, delicious food and drink, the amusements of the coliseum, and the pleasures of sexual relationships. On the outside, Augustine appeared to have it all. But on the inside, he had an ache in his heart. Something was missing.

Augustine eventually came to see that, while there is nothing wrong with experiencing in moderation and in the proper way the good things of this world—money, success, sex, power—these things cannot fulfill us. God made us with "longings for the infinite",[12] and nothing from this finite world can satisfy us. Only the infinite God can fulfill the deepest desires of our hearts. That's why Augustine concluded in his famous prayer to God, "You have made us for yourself, and our hearts are restless until they rest in you."[13]

What Do You Seek First?

Long before Augustine offered that prayer, he had come to believe in God, but God was not at the center of his life. Other things were more important to him: honor, praise, worldly entertainments, sex. He believed in God, but he

---

[12] *CCC* 33.
[13] Augustine, *Confessions* 1, 1.

sought his happiness in other things and did not follow God's plan for his life.

When we, like early Augustine, search for our security, fulfillment, and happiness in anything short of God, we, too, will experience anxiety, frustration, and lack of peace. If we don't put God first—if we make God just one of the many things in our lives—we will never be truly happy. Our hearts will be restless.

The ideas discussed in this chapter—God's existence as the Trinity and our being made in the "image" of the triune God—challenge us to ask ourselves the following: What is really most important in my life? For whom do I really live? Do I live more for God and others or more for myself? Do I live like the Trinity, a life of self-giving? Or do I live seeking my fulfillment in the things of this world?

In the rest of this book, we will see that the Catholic faith is a whole way of life. The various aspects of the faith—Jesus, the Bible, the Church, the saints, the sacraments, morality, and prayer—are not just religious ideas or abstract doctrines. They have everything to do with our day-to-day life. They are all about our encounter with the God who is love. And they help us live more deeply with him at the center of our lives. Think of all the facets of the Catholic faith as lights guiding us on the path to personal fulfillment, the path that leads us to God—the triune God, in whom alone our hearts find rest.

Chapter Two

The Divine Unveiling

Religion is sometimes thought of as mankind's search for God. But Christianity is more about God's search for us. God didn't just create us. He didn't leave us on our own to find him and discover the meaning of our existence. Love desires to be near the beloved, and the God who is love sought us out and entered into our world. He spoke to his people through his prophets, his law, and his Scriptures, and even by becoming one of us in Jesus Christ.

Here we see that Christians don't just believe in God. We believe that the God of the universe lovingly chose to unveil himself to us and show us his plan for our lives. And that personal self-disclosure of God is what we call "divine revelation".

But for many people today, the idea of a God in heaven communicating to us on earth seems like something from ancient myths and fairy tales. Does God *really* speak to us through prophets, leaders, and inspired biblical writers? And what makes divine revelation in the Christian tradition different from the religious teachings found in other religions of the world? And finally, how does God reveal himself, and where can we find this revelation today? These are some of the questions we will explore in this chapter.

St. Paul, Basilica of St. Paul Outside the Walls, Rome

From the *Symbolon* series

Does God Really Communicate to Us?

It is somewhat understandable that many people in our culture don't believe God communicates to us. Many people today are influenced by a popular notion of God known as deism—the belief in a spectator God, a God who created the universe, gave it order, but then just sit backs and watches us from a distance. According to the deistic perspective, God exists, but he is not involved in this world. God does not perform miracles. He does not know our thoughts. He does not hear our prayers. He does not help us in our need and certainly doesn't desire a personal relationship with us. So if someone is not convinced there is a God who really interacts with us in the world, he is not going to be very open to the possibility that God reveals himself to us through Jesus, the Bible, or the Church.

But is this deistic view reasonable? Does it make sense to say that God does not interact in this world?

First, if there is a God who created the universe, surely he would at least have the *ability* to enter into the work of his own creation. It would be foolish to say that a builder, for example, would be incapable of entering into the building he himself constructed. Similarly, it is unreasonable to say that God, the divine architect of the cosmos, could not enter into his own creation and interact with the people therein. We should, therefore, be open at least to the fact that God has the *ability* to be involved in his creation, influence affairs of this world, know our needs, answer our prayers, and even reveal himself and his plan for our lives. It would be quite unreasonable to say that it is *impossible* for God to interact in his own creation and reveal himself to his people.

Still, we can go further. Not only does God have the ability to communicate to us, but it makes a lot of sense that he would choose to do so. We need God's help to understand who he is and what his plan is for our lives. The medieval theologian Saint Thomas Aquinas explains how we, with our finite minds, cannot comprehend the infinite God on our own.[1] After all, many of us have a hard enough time wrapping our minds around subjects such as calculus, biochemistry, or astrophysics. If we experience our mind's limitations in grasping earthly subjects like these, how much more so we will struggle to understand fully the Almighty God. Therefore, if God wants us to know him and love him, it is fitting that he would reveal himself to us.

Aren't All Religions the Same?

It is sometimes said that each individual's religious views are like different roads leading up the same mountain to God.

---

[1] St. Thomas Aquinas, *Summa Theologica* I, q. 1, art. 1.

No one road is better than another. It is just assumed that God didn't give any special revelation about who he is and what he expects from us. So, any claim that one religion has more to offer the world than others is viewed as arrogant and narrow-minded.

Such a perspective might have some merit if all the roads between us and God were man-made. But Christians do not believe in a passive, uninvolved God who leaves us completely on our own to climb up to him and figure him out. As we've seen, Christians believe in a God who loves us—a God who personally came to us, revealed himself to us, and showed us the true path to happiness. Indeed, Christians believe that God himself came down from heaven and became one of us, forging the road between God and man. In the words of Catholic writer Peter Kreeft, "there is no human way up the mountain, only a divine way down."[2] After all, if there is a God who loves us, doesn't it seem likely that he would come to us and show us the best path to him? Kreeft goes on to challenge the modern "all roads are the same" mentality: "If God made the road, we must find out whether he made many or one. If he made only one, then the shoe is on the other foot: it is humility, not arrogance, to accept this one road from God; and it is arrogance, not humility, to insist that our man-made roads are as good as God's God-made one."[3]

We should at least consider the possibility that God may have taken the trouble to reveal himself to us and show us his plan for our lives. This, after all, is what Jesus claimed. He said he is "the way, and the truth, and the life" and that no one can come to the Father except through him (Jn 14:6).

[2] Peter Kreeft, *Fundamentals of the Faith* (San Francisco: Ignatius Press, 1988), 76.

[3] Ibid., 77.

From the *Symbolon* series

St. John with his Gospel, St. Peter's Basilica, Vatican City

If Jesus truly is the way to the Father, that's something we would want to take into consideration for our lives!

This does not mean that the other religions of the world contain no truth. The *Catechism* makes very clear that God can work outside the visible confines of the Catholic Church, and that there are elements of truth found in the other religions of the world. But, as we will see later, Catholics believe that the fullness of God's revelation was given in Jesus Christ and has been passed on to us today through his Church (see *CCC* 819).

Another thing that makes Christian revelation unique is that in other religions, the emphasis is on ethical rules, principles for life, and ideas about God and his will for us. In Christianity, however, the focus is on God revealing *himself.*

Whatever doctrines or moral principles that may flow from God's revelation are ultimately at the service of knowing and loving him. In fact, the word the early Christians used to describe God's communication tells us a lot about the very *personal* nature of divine revelation: *apokalupsis*, a Greek word that can be translated "unveiling". Like a bride unveiling herself to her husband, so God unveils himself to us so that we can respond to him in love.

God is not interested in merely downloading important information to us about the Christian life. He lovingly unveils his very self to us, so that we can love him back. "By revealing himself God wishes to make them capable of responding to him, and of knowing him, and of loving him far beyond their own natural capacity" (*CCC* 52).

Where Do We Find God's Revelation Today?

More than twenty centuries ago, in a small outpost of the Roman Empire known as Nazareth of Galilee, God entered human history in the most profound way. In the womb of a virgin, the Son of God became man in Jesus Christ. Or, as the Gospel of Saint John says, the divine Word of God "became flesh and dwelt among us" (Jn 1:14).

God had been preparing mankind, especially his people Israel, for the coming of his Son, gradually revealing himself to people like Abraham, Moses, David, and various prophets, disclosing a little more of himself at each step of the way. This gradual unveiling of God reached its climax with Jesus. As we will see more in chapter 5, Jesus is not just a prophet, teacher, or messenger sent from God. He is God himself, who has become man. "In many and various ways God spoke of old to our fathers by the prophets; but in these last days he has spoken to us by a Son" (Heb 1:1–2). Jesus, therefore, is the fullness of God's revelation.

As the God-Man, Jesus gathered disciples, proclaimed a kingdom, and called people to believe in him to have eternal life. Jesus revealed himself as "the way, and the truth, and the life", offering the true path for the entire family of mankind to find fullness of life in God. Since Jesus was God become man, everything about his life—his teaching, his example, his training of his disciples—reveals who God is. Indeed, in Jesus we find the fullness of God's unveiling of himself.

But that was more than two thousand years ago. How do we today come to know all that Jesus revealed?

After teaching and training his disciples for three years, Jesus commissioned them to pass on all that he taught them to the rest of the world for all generations. Before ascending into heaven, Jesus told his apostles, "Go therefore and make disciples of all nations, baptizing them in the name of the Father and of the Son and of the Holy Spirit, teaching them to observe all that I have commanded you" (Mt 28:19–20). The apostles and their successors carried out this instruction, known as the Great Commission, by handing on all that Jesus revealed. They did this in two ways: in writing and in oral form (see *CCC* 76). The written manner of passing on the gospel refers to Sacred Scripture, while the oral form is called Sacred Tradition.

Sacred Scripture

First, one of the main ways we can come to know God's revelation is through Sacred Scripture.

Some of the apostles and their associates put Christ's message of salvation into writing. Texts such as the Gospels of Matthew, Mark, Luke, and John and the letters of Saint Paul were recognized by the early Church as being not just any ordinary texts but writings inspired by God himself. And those writings became part of the New Testament books of the Bible. Christians speak of these texts, along with the Old Testament books of the Bible, as truly being "inspired by God" (2 Tim 3:16).

But what does this mean?

The word "inspiration" in English is based on the Greek word *theopneustos*, which means "God-breathed". The inspiration of the Bible refers to how the Holy Spirit influenced writers such as Saint Paul to write, not just their own words, but God's words. In the Bible, God "breathed" his own divine words through the words of men.

This doesn't mean that the Bible magically floated down from heaven or that God mechanically forced men to write certain words on a page like robots. The writers of Scripture acted as true authors. They wrote in an ordinary human way, making full use of their own freedom, creativity, and writing styles, and having their original audience in mind throughout the process. But these authors were also guided by the Holy Spirit so that, as the *Catechism* explains, "they consigned to writing whatever he wanted written, and no more."[4]

Here we see the mystery of inspiration: the biblical texts were written by men, but they have God as author as well. While the human writers were free to write whatever they wanted, what they wrote is exactly what God wanted written "and no more".

---

[4] *CCC* 106, citing Vatican II, Dogmatic Constitution on Divine Revelation, *Dei Verbum*, November 18, 1965, no. 11.

The Bible, therefore, consists not just of human words but of the Word of God in the words of men. In Scripture, we don't just read about stories from a long time ago. We encounter the living God speaking to us through the biblical texts today. "For in the sacred books, the Father who is in heaven meets his children with great love and speaks with them."[5]

Sacred Tradition

The second way we can come to know God's revelation in Christ is through Sacred Tradition.

One biblical theme to help us understand more accurately what Catholics mean by Sacred Tradition is that of discipleship. The word "disciple" means "student", but we shouldn't think of modern students in a classroom merely sitting and listening to the teacher's lessons. Jewish rabbis gathered disciples and invited them into an apprenticeship of sorts, a participation in their whole way of life. They trained their disciples not primarily through lectures or written texts, but by their example. At the heart of discipleship is imitation of the master's life.

Jesus, like other rabbis of his day, gathered disciples and invited them to participate in his life. He didn't say to them, "Come, listen to my lecture on the Lord's Prayer", but rather, "Follow me."[6] Indeed, the disciples actually followed Jesus from village to village; they lived with him, prayed with him, shared meals with him, and served the sick and the poor with him. Every day, the disciples observed the way Jesus prayed, the way he preached, and the way he helped those in need. They witnessed him reach out to sinners, defend his

---

[5] *Dei Verbum*, no. 21.
[6] Mt 4:19; Mk 1:17; see Lk 5:11 and Jn 1:37.

Inspiration of St. Matthew, Caravaggio, Church of San Luigi de Francesi, Rome

teaching to the Pharisees, have compassion on the suffering, and call people to repent.

By accompanying Christ for three years, the disciples assimilated not just Jesus' teachings, but his whole way of living—not just what they learned "from the lips of Christ", but also "his way of life and his works" (*CCC* 76). So when it came time for their own preaching of the gospel, the apostles passed on all that they had taken in from their discipleship with Jesus and from their continued guidance by the Holy Spirit.[7] The *Catechism* explains that they passed on the gospel "by the spoken word of their preaching,[8] by the example

---

[7]See *CCC* 76. Jesus promised the apostles that the Holy Spirit would "teach you all things, and bring to your remembrance all that I have said to you" (Jn 14:26). So even after Jesus ascended to heaven, the promised Spirit continued to guide the apostles throughout their lives into an ever deeper understanding of the mystery of Christ.

[8]See Acts 2:14–36; 3:1–11; 5:42; 7:1–53.

they gave,[9] [and] by the institutions they established",[10] such as baptism, the Eucharist, a council, and appointed presbyters who shared in their mission.[11] It is this living transmission of the Christian life that is at the heart of Sacred Tradition.

The *Catechism* identifies four main "places" where we today come in touch with this work of the Holy Spirit in Sacred Tradition:

1. In the Church's doctrine, as found in the creeds, Church councils, the *Catechism*, magisterial teaching, and the theological and spiritual writers who are recognized as model teachers in the Catholic Church.

2. In the Church's life, as seen in the lives of the saints, popular devotions, religious movements, and common practices that have gained wide acceptance in the Church.

3. In the Church's worship, as found in the liturgy, sacraments, feasts, prayers, sacred music, and art.

4. In the early Church leaders and theologians known as the Church Fathers, who are principal witnesses to Sacred Tradition because of their proximity to the time of the apostles and the way their writings helped organize and deepen the Church's understanding of the apostolic faith.

Magisterium

Finally, Jesus didn't just offer the world his teaching and then leave people on their own to interpret it however they please.

[9] See Acts 2:42–47; 4:23–37; 6:1–6.

[10] *CCC* 76, citing *Dei Verbum*, no. 7.

[11] Baptism: Acts 2:38–41; 8:38; 10:48; the Eucharist: Acts 2:42; 20:7; a council: Acts 15:2–29; presbyters who shared in the apostles' mission: Acts 15:4, 6, 23; 20:17, 28–29.

One can imagine the confusion and division that would result if each individual believer was only given a book or a set of traditions to figure out for himself. Instead of being a united body of believers, Christ's followers would be divided, each interpreting Christ's teachings in his own way. This is one reason why Jesus wisely established a Church to help us accurately understand his teachings and apply them to our lives. He gave his apostles teaching authority, so that they might serve as the authentic interpreters of his revelation (see Mt 16:18–20; 18:18).

Christ's revelation in Scripture and Tradition, therefore, was entrusted to the Church's teaching authority called the Magisterium (from the Latin word *magister*, meaning "teacher"), which serves as the divinely appointed guardian and interpreter of all that has been passed on from Jesus and the apostles to the present day. The Magisterium consists of the successors of the apostles (the bishops) teaching in union with the successor of Saint Peter (the pope). As we will see more in chapter 7, Jesus gave the apostles authority to teach in his name, and that authority was passed on to their successors, the bishops, throughout the centuries. The Magisterium is not a separate source of divine revelation, but a great gift for us to help us know and live out God's revelation contained in Scripture and Tradition. Guided by the Holy Spirit, the "Magisterium is not superior to the word of God but is its servant", guarding it and expounding on it faithfully (*CCC* 86).

Is the Bible Alone Enough?

While the Catholic Church reveres the Bible as the inspired Word of God and the very soul of sacred theology, many

Protestant Christians hold to the idea of *sola scriptura* (Scripture alone). This is the belief that Scripture is the *only* infallible authority for the Christian faith. In this view, there is no need for Sacred Tradition or an authoritative Church. The Bible is the only thing we need if we want to know what God has revealed.

The Catholic understanding of divine revelation, however, is different. The Bible is one important way Christians come to know God's revelation, but it was never the only way. And it was never intended to be read individualistically outside the community of faith from which it arose. In short, Catholics, while affirming the noble love and reverence for Scripture that our Protestant brethren have, would see three main challenges with the view that Scripture is the *only* source of divine revelation: *sola scriptura* is unbiblical, unhistorical, and unworkable.

First, the very notion of *sola scriptura* itself is, ironically, opposed to what the Bible actually teaches. Scripture nowhere says that the Bible is the only source of divine authority. The Bible itself reveals that there was something more than written texts that were to be passed on from Jesus' apostles to us today. For example, long before the New Testament was even written, the apostles already were commissioned to make disciples of all nations, baptizing them and teaching them all that Jesus had taught them (see Mt 28:18–20). They already were preaching the gospel, calling people to repent, to follow Jesus, and to live the Christian life. The earliest Christians in Jerusalem gathered to hear the apostles' oral teachings, and they were united in fellowship, the Eucharist, and prayer (see Acts 2:42). And they did all this without any of the written New Testament texts. The very idea of *sola scriptura* would not have made sense to the earliest Christians. Moreover, the Bible emphasizes that we must hold on to the oral traditions of the apostles, not just what was kept

From the Symbolon series

St. Peter, St. Peter's Basilica, Vatican City

in writing. As Saint Paul taught, "So then, brethren, stand firm and hold to the traditions which you were taught by us, either by word of mouth or by letter" (2 Thess 2:15). *Sola scriptura* is an *unbiblical* belief.

Second, *sola scriptura* is unhistorical. It is something that no Christian held for the first fourteen hundred years of the Church. Up until the eve of the Protestant Reformation, Christians had always read Scripture within the context of the living Church and in light of Sacred Tradition. The idea of taking Scripture out of that context and claiming it as the only source of divine revelation was a departure from the way Christians had been reading Scripture since the time of the apostles.

Third, *sola scriptura* is unworkable. God didn't simply give us a sacred book and then leave us completely on our own to interpret it. God gave us a Church to help us understand the Scriptures and apply them to our lives. But imagine the chaos if everyone started interpreting the Bible all on his own, coming up with his own doctrines, moral principles, and applications based on his personal reading of Scripture and claiming that the Holy Spirit led him to these conclusions. Yet, that's what *sola scriptura* does. It is an individualistic approach to the Bible in which someone says, "I don't need the Church or Tradition. I just need the Bible, and God will show me what the Bible means."

This approach, however, is practically unworkable. With each individual deciding for himself what the Bible means, *sola scriptura* only leads to further divisions within Christianity. In fact, since the time Martin Luther promoted the idea of *sola scriptura* in the sixteenth century, thousands of divisions have been sown in the body of Christ with rival Christian groups, each disagreeing with each other on the meaning of the Bible and each claiming that the Holy Spirit is guiding them to the correct interpretation. As a result, there are today tens of thousands of different Christian denominations. With each individual deciding for himself what the Bible means, *sola scriptura* can only lead to further divisions within Christianity.

* * * * *

In conclusion, we have seen three key elements related to divine revelation: Scripture, Tradition, and the Magisterium. Like the three legs of a stool, each is necessary to know and understand what God has revealed to us. No one piece can stand on its own. As Vatican II taught, "It is clear therefore that, in the supremely wise arrangement of God, sacred Tradition, Sacred Scripture, and the Magisterium of the Church are so connected and associated that one of them cannot stand without the others. Working together, each in its own way, under the action of the one Holy Spirit, they all contribute effectively to the salvation of souls."[12]

---

[12] *CCC* 95, citing *Dei Verbum*, no. 10.

Chapter Three

The Great Story

What do we do with a movie that's going nowhere? What do we do with a book that has no plot? We put the book down. We turn off the movie. When we sense there's no meaning, no purpose, to the story, it seems pointless to go on.

The same is true with life.

Our modern world has, in many ways, lost its story. We no longer know where we came from. We don't know where we're going. And we don't know why we're here.

But God has a wonderful plan for our lives, one in which we discover the true, lasting happiness for which we are made. And the Creed, which Christians have been reciting since the time of the early Church, is a short retelling of that saving plan. This ancient summary statement of Christian faith provides a framework for our lives. It reminds us from where we came: "I believe in one God the Father Almighty, Creator of heaven and earth". It points to where we're going: "I look forward to the resurrection of the dead and the life of the world to come". And it shows us why we're here: for a relationship with the God who loves us so much that "for us men and for our salvation, he came down from heaven".

The Creed reinforces how our individual lives are part of a much larger story—a story that has been going on since the dawn of creation. Like most good stories, it involves a

Santo Spiritu in Sassia Church, interior, Vatican City

struggle between good and evil, love and loss, life and death. The rest of this book, indeed the entirety of the Catholic faith, is all about this story and the important role you and I are called to play in it.

But before we delve into the details, let's step back and rediscover the big picture of this story, which is compelling not only for its beauty, but most of all, because it is true. In fact, the best stories in the world are, in the end, reflections or variations of this one true story that provides the proper lens for seeing reality. It is only by viewing our lives in context of this much larger narrative that we begin to discover the plan God has for our lives.

* * * * *

Some of the most important things that God brought into existence cannot be seen with human eyes.

When we think about God's creation, we must envision more than beautiful mountains, valleys, rivers, and oceans. The Lord's handiwork also involves much more than the flowers, trees, animals, and people that fill the earth. To grasp God's creation adequately, we even have to look beyond the sun, moon, stars, and galaxies that make up the universe. The opening line of Scripture draws our attention to God's creating beings that are greater than anything else in the entire cosmos: "In the beginning God created the *heavens*" (Gen 1:1; emphasis added).

"The heavens" here refers to the spiritual beings God created first: the angels. Though we can't see them, angels are more magnificent than the peak of Mount Everest, the depths of the ocean, or the stars of the Milky Way galaxy. And they are superior to mankind in knowledge, power, and glory. Like us, each angel exists as an individual person with its own mind and free will. But unlike men and women, angels do not have bodies. They are purely spiritual beings, beyond the physical realm, and thus cannot be seen. Though they intervene in our world all the time, their presence is beyond the reach of our senses.

God made the angels to know and love him, to glorify him, and to serve him in the world he was about to create. But God gave the angels free will and did not force them to serve. He gave them a choice. Before they could see God "face-to-face" and be sent on their mission, their love was tested in some way.

Scripture does not specify the nature of the test, but we do know that many of the angels fared well. Many saw the sheer goodness of their God—a God who did not need to create them or anything else, and yet freely chose to bring them into existence to share his goodness, love, and power with them. In awe and wonder over God's goodness to them, these angels responded in love. They chose to serve and adore their God.

Many of these angels are described in the Bible as the "myriads and myriads"—the thousands and tens of thousands—who worship God (see Dan 7:10). These are the angels whom Jesus says "behold the face" of his heavenly Father (Mt 18:10). These angels serve as his messengers, assist God in implementing his will on earth (see Ps 102:20), and encourage, guard, and protect us in our daily lives (cf. Mt 18:10).

There was one angel, however, who stood out among all the rest. The early Christians called him the "light bearer" or "shining one". The description points to how glorious this particular angel must have been. It is traditionally believed that God invested more of his glory, power, and strength in this angel than in any other. What a beautiful sight it must have been to gaze upon the "shining one" who reflected God's glory the most!

But this angel viewed his splendor as his own, not as a reflection of God's. He did not want to bow down before his Creator, but focused on himself. Blind to God's goodness and love and so caught up by his own magnificence, he had a false sense of self-sufficiency, as if all his shining qualities were his own and not a gift from God. He ignored God's supremacy, rejected God, and sought to build a kingdom for himself.[1] This is the angel whom the Bible calls "Satan" or "the devil" (Rev 12:9). He is described in Scripture as the "prince of demons" (Mt 12:24; see Mt 12:25–32) and ruler

---

[1] See John Paul II, *God, Father and Creator: A Catechesis on the Creed*, vol. 1 (Boston: Daughters of St. Paul, 1996), 296–97, from his "General Audience", July 23, 1986.

of the world enslaved by sin (see Jn 12:31), for he led many other angels to join his rebellion against God (see 2 Pet 1:4; Jude 1:6; Job 4:18). Many Christians today know this angel as "Lucifer", for Lucifer means "light bearer".

Think about that. The devil actually thought he could gain independence from his Creator. And he convinced many other angels of that lie as well. How powerfully seductive Satan is in leading others to rebel against God! Though Satan, along with the other fallen angels, was cast out of heaven, he made it his goal to wage war against God in any way that he could. Satan knows he cannot destroy God, but he could destroy God's children. He eventually set his eyes on the family of mankind in the visible world God would create. Perhaps he could convince them to join in his rebellion as well.

Man and Woman: The Crowning of God's Creation

It has been said that God left his fingerprints on everything he created. This is especially true for his crowning work: man and woman. God brought into existence the earth, sky, and sea; the sun, moon, and stars; the birds, fish, and animals— but the Scriptures tell us he made only man and woman specifically in his own image and likeness. They reflected God more than anything else in the visible world.

How so? God, who is all-knowing and all-loving, gave man and woman a share in his own ability to know and to love. He gave them a mind to know, and a free will with the power to choose and to love. Capable of self-knowledge and of freely giving themselves to others, man and woman can enter into communion with each other and even with God.

As such, individual persons can do something that nothing else in the entire visible world can do: know and love their Creator (see *CCC* 356–57).

In the beginning, man and woman lived in a profound unity of love—a union on earth that reflected the very unity of God himself: the Holy Trinity. Man and woman were, first of all, in right relationship with God, filled with his life and love. And they lived in right relationship with each other and in perfect harmony with the rest of the earth. There was no sin, no sorrow, no suffering, no death. Man and woman were completely happy. That's why, after creating man and woman this way, God saw that "[i]t was very good" (Gen 1:31).

The Fall

But not everyone was happy seeing God's love manifested on earth. Satan and the fallen angels hated God and all the good he was doing in the world. Though they were cast out of heaven, they could invade the visible realm and oppose God there. They could break up the unity of the human family by convincing our first parents to join their rebellion. Satan tempted man and woman not to trust God's goodness and to seek a greater glory and power for themselves. We find a reflection of the devil's own prideful rebellion in his enticing words to them in the garden: "[Y]ou will be like God" (Gen 3:5). Satan wasn't just trying to get Adam and Eve to break a rule. He was trying to break a relationship. At its heart, the first sin was about Adam and Eve in their pride refusing to love the God who was so good to them and rejecting God's plan of goodness for their lives. Like Satan and the fallen angels, man and woman wanted to be "like God" but

From the *Symbolon* series

Adam and Eve, Vatican Museums, Vatican City

without God, and they refused to give themselves to him in love (see *CCC* 397–98).

This first sin had tragic consequences. The Bible describes how Adam and Eve immediately turned away and hid themselves from the Lord (see Gen 3:10), signifying how they turned away from the Lord in their sin and are now separated from him.

But they also found that in their separation from God they had also broken their relationship with each other and with the rest of creation. Man and woman suddenly lived in tension with each other and became subject to suffering and death. Instead of unity and order, mankind is now fraught with division and chaos. Satan could claim a victory. He succeeded in turning the united family of God into the divided family of man, with God's children separated from their heavenly Father and at war with each other.

Moreover, without the supernatural gift of God's life in us, the members of the human family ever since have had a wounded human nature, an "inclination to evil" (*CCC* 405). It is no longer easy for us to do what is good. Our minds don't always see what is true and good clearly, and our wills are weakened. Even when we know what we should do, we often fail to do it. Saint Paul describes this inner struggle in his letter to the Romans: "I do not do what I want, but I do the very thing I hate.... I do not do the good I want, but the evil I do not want is what I do" (Rom 7:15, 19).

This is how the devil took some control in God's good and orderly world. Satan found a welcome home in the hearts of men and women. Man still has free will, but as a result of the first sin, Satan has gained a certain dominion over the human family. Wounded by this original sin and inclined to what is sinful, man's life is now an inner battle between good and evil (see *CCC* 409).

It would be reasonable and even just if God abandoned Adam and Eve for having rejected him. Yet, God's first response is not wrath, but mercy. He still loved them, sought them out, and announced his plan to rescue them. Though there would be consequences of the original sin and an ongoing struggle between good and evil, God unveils his plan of salvation. He foretold of someone he would send, a descendant of the woman, who would defeat the devil and liberate us from his dominion of sin and death (see Gen 3:15).

God's Rescue Mission

It is an astonishing fact that the all-good God chose to enter our world to rescue us. Though we were sinners who rejected his love in a thousand ways, he ardently pursued us to bring us back into union with him. He became one of us in Jesus Christ, the God-Man.

And the *way* he came to save us is just as remarkable. He didn't enter our world as a king coming on a throne or as a powerful ruler riding in a chariot with his army. He came as a baby to the small city of Bethlehem, an obscure outpost on the edge of the Roman Empire. And with such humble beginnings, the arrival of the Son of God escapes the notice of almost everyone in the world.

But the devil knew something was happening. He did not like this newborn child and wanted to have him killed. All the male children two years old and younger near Bethlehem were massacred by a wicked king named Herod. But an angel of the Lord intervened, warning Jesus' adoptive father, Joseph, of the threat and telling him to take the child to Egypt for safety (see Matt 2:13–18).

Thirty years later, when the adult Jesus is about to launch his ministry and announce the kingdom of God coming to men, the devil shows up again (see Mt 4:1–11; Mk 1:12–13; Lk 4:1–13). This time, he tries to tempt Jesus just as he had tempted Adam and Eve. But Jesus outwits Satan and remains faithful to his heavenly Father. The devil can't lead Jesus into sin as he did our first parents.

Finally, the devil unleashes his most severe attack on Jesus by getting the rulers of the world to conspire against him and even prompting one of Jesus' own disciples to betray him (see Lk 22:52–53; Jn 13:27). Jesus is nailed to the cross by the Romans and killed on Good Friday. The world turns dark. Jesus' body is buried in a tomb. And it appears that Satan has won in the end.

But that's not the whole of the story.

Jesus is not a passive victim. He is the Almighty God, the Lord of lords, King of kings, and master of the universe.

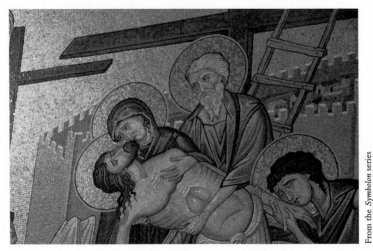

Church of the Holy Sepulcher, interior, Jerusalem

From the *Symbolon* series

He did not go to his Crucifixion against his will. In an instant he could have called on his angels to rescue him. Or he could have escaped his executioners by his own divine power. But Jesus, the Son of God, loved us so much that he did the most unexpected thing: he freely chose to give up his life for our sake, so that we could be reunited with him. And that's what love does. It drives us to the most surprising levels of generosity, service, and sacrifice. The God who is love—the God who was so passionately in love with us and so desired to be united to us—was even willing to lay down his life for us. As Saint Catherine of Siena once said, the nails could not have held Jesus to the cross if love had not held him there first.[2]

---

[2] See Vida D. Scudder, trans., *Saint Catherine of Siena as Seen in Her Letters* (London: J.M. Dent, 1906), p. 42.

And then the most astonishing thing happened: the greatest miracle in the history of the world. Jesus rose from the dead on the third day. Ever since the fall, the human family has been under Satan's dominion and trapped in the bonds of death. But Satan had no hold over Jesus. He could not seduce Jesus into sin, and he could not keep Jesus trapped in death. In the resurrected Jesus lies our hope. Jesus goes before us, the firstborn from the dead, and we who share in Christ's life will rise with him on the last day.

How Christ's death and Resurrection save us from sin will be discussed more in chapter 6. Suffice it to say here that, because of sin, an infinite chasm was introduced between God and man—a chasm that only the infinite God could bridge. But since sin entered the world through man, a man is responsible to do something: to perform an act of great love to make reconciliation and restore right relationship with God. Therefore, God entered our humanity and became one of us so that he could represent us and offer a truly human act of love on our behalf. And since Jesus is God, his sacrificial death on the cross takes on infinite value and undoes the knot of sin. Through the death and Resurrection of Jesus, man and woman can be in a right relationship with God again.

But how do we come to share in Christ's life and his victory over sin and death? How do we receive all that Christ won for us in his death and Resurrection? In short, through the outpouring of the Holy Spirit on the Church.

The Holy Spirit and the Church

Ever since the fall, Satan has sown division in the world. But God's plan from the very beginning was for us to be united in love with him and with each other. That's why after the first sin God gradually began gathering his people back together, working with the family of Abraham, the nation of Israel, and the wider kingdom of David to prepare them for the coming of his Son, Jesus. God's plan of salvation was for us not just to be reunited with him, but also to be restored to unity with each other. So important was the unity of God's people that, on the night before Jesus died, he prayed that all Christians would be one, even as he and the Father are one (see Jn 17).

This plan for unity took a major step forward at the event known as Pentecost (see Acts 2:1–42). In the fullness of his Resurrection triumph, after ascending to his Father in heaven, Jesus poured out his Spirit onto the Church. Filled with the Holy Spirit, Jesus' apostles proclaimed the gospel in Jerusalem, and three thousand people repented and were baptized in a single day. These new believers were among the first to receive the Holy Spirit and be reconciled to God and brought into unity with each other through their new shared life in Christ. As such, they were among the first in the world to be gathered back into the reunited family of God, the Church.

Jesus entrusted this ministry of reconciliation to twelve of his closest associates, known as the twelve apostles. He commissioned them to carry on his ministry in two main ways.

First, Jesus gave the apostles authority to *teach* all nations all that he had taught them (see Mt 28:19–20). Jesus had revealed to them the truth about God and the true path to happiness and salvation. He exhorted them to live the way they were made to live—for self-giving love, like God himself—and not the way of self-assertion exhibited by the devil.

But Jesus needed the apostles to do more than proclaim the truth to us. Simply *knowing* the truth does not mean we will be able to live it out. We've seen how we're fallen, wounded by original sin. Our selfish, fearful, prideful hearts need to be healed. That's why Jesus gave the apostles a second mission: to *baptize* "in the name of the Father and of the Son and of the Holy Spirit" (Mt 28:19).

Through baptism, we receive the Holy Spirit into our souls. The God of the universe comes to dwells within us, reconciling us to the Father! Here we see that Jesus didn't just teach us about self-giving love, and he didn't just give us an example of perfect love. He actually wants to *reproduce* his love in us through sending his Spirit into our hearts so that we can live like him.

Jesus does this work in us most especially through baptism and the other sacraments of the Church. Through the sacraments, Christ fills us with his Spirit, deepens our union with God, and enables us to love far beyond what we could do by our own natural power. On our own, it would be impossible to love as Christ has loved us. But Christ's Spirit changes us. Our hardened hearts are softened, and we are gradually transformed by his love, so that we can begin to say with Saint Paul, "[I]t is no longer I who live, but Christ who lives in me" (Gal 2:20). It is in this way that God continues to drive back the devil and extends his kingdom on earth, step-by-step, from one small act of human love to another. And the more we cooperate with Christ's Spirit, the more God molds us into souls fully taken over by his love—that is, the more we become saints, true heroes in this story.

Entering the Story

This is the great drama that has been going on since the dawn of creation: a struggle between good and evil, between the God of love and the "shining one" who wanted to usurp all glory and power for himself. And we already know how

Shutterstock

Basilica of St. Paul Outside the Wall, interior, Rome

this story will end: "Christ will come to judge the living and the dead." The risen Jesus will come on the last day to set all things right, make all things new, and invite his faithful servants to share in eternal life with him.

It is our turn now to enter the story. The question is, how well will we play our part? Will we help extend God's kingdom on earth? Or will we assist the enemy in opposing God's plan for love and unity? Will we follow the way of Jesus? Or will we imitate the way of our first parents? Will we pursue the way of love or the way of self? As the *Catechism* explains, "The whole of man's history has been the story of our combat with the powers of evil, stretching, so our Lord tells us, from the very dawn of history until the last day. Finding himself in the midst of the battlefield man has to struggle to do what is right, and it is at great cost to himself, and aided by God's grace, that he succeeds in achieving his own inner integrity."[3]

If you want to give the best of yourself to God in this drama, then the rest of this book is for you. For as we walk through the faith, we will see that everything about Catholic beliefs and Catholic living—whether it be about Jesus, the Church, Mary, the sacraments, sex, care for the poor or prayer—*everything* is centered on our relationship with Jesus and helps us live more profoundly in his love and radiate his love more in the world. And the more we live according to God's plan for our lives, the more we will resist the enemy, help build up Christ's kingdom on earth and make our lives, as Blessed Mother Teresa of Calcutta liked to say, "something beautiful for God".

[3] *CCC* 409, quoting Vatican II, Pastoral Constitution on the Church in the Modern World, *Gaudium et Spes*, December 7, 1965, no. 37.

Chapter Four

"Who Do You Say That I Am?"

When staring at early artistic depictions of Christ, such as the one featured in the Basilica of Saints Cosmas and Damian in Rome, one is confronted by a startling Christian claim about Jesus.

In this sixth-century mosaic, Jesus appears with a toga of an ancient philosopher and a raised arm in the gesture of a teacher. But he is not just another religious guru or wise sage. Light radiating from his golden robes signifies Jesus' divinity. And he comes on the fiery clouds, a biblical image that points to Jesus as the divine Lord announcing the Last Judgment. Jesus "will come again to judge the living and the dead."

This was one of the first Christian churches built right in the center of ancient Rome, amid the various pagan shrines that fell into disuse. The arresting image of Christ would have challenged the Romans back then to see in Jesus much more than a spiritual leader. It proclaims Jesus as the divine Lord over heaven and earth. And the mosaic challenges us today to make a similar choice about Christ: Will Jesus be for us merely a wise teacher, just one of many spiritual guides throughout history who have offered a path to God? Or will we see in Jesus something utterly unique, something that makes him different from any other religious leader the world has ever known?

From the Symbolon series

Basilica of Sts. Cosmas and Damian, interior, Rome

More Than a Good Man

At the very heart of Christianity is not an idea, but a Person: Jesus Christ, the eternal Son of God who became man. The Bible describes how Jesus "came forth from God" (Jn 8:42), "descended from heaven" (Jn 3:19), and "came in the flesh" (2 Jn 1:7). Christians call this mystery of God becoming man the Incarnation—literally, the "enfleshment" of the divine Son of God, who took on human nature in order to accomplish his work of salvation. Christians believe Jesus is truly God and truly man. God loved us so much that he became one of us to reconcile us to the Father, reveal his love, serve as a model for holiness, and share his divine life with us (see *CCC* 1056–60). What a profound mystery this is! The infinite, all-holy, almighty God of heaven and earth actually humbled himself, entered our world, and became one of us in Jesus Christ!

Many people today, however, view Jesus as just a good man—a moral teacher, a political leader, and someone who cared for the poor and taught us to love. But the inescapable fact is that Jesus claimed to be so much more. He acted and spoke in the Person of God. And if one understands the Jewish culture of Jesus' day, it's clear he did so boldly.

We see this in the way he forgave people's sins, which was something only God could do. A Jewish man might forgive someone for hurting him, but he doesn't have the power to forgive others for all the sins they've ever committed against God. Only God can do that. Yet, it was this all-encompassing forgiveness of sins that Jesus offered people throughout his public ministry. And this was shocking to his contemporaries. When he said, for example, to a paralyzed man, "[Y]our sins are forgiven you," the scribes and Pharisees were scandalized and accused Jesus of blasphemy. They asked, "Who can forgive sins but God only?" (Lk 5:20–21).

Jesus also asserted divine authority in his teaching. In his famous Sermon on the Mount, he spoke about God's law in a startling way that no one had ever done before. The Jews believed that the law (the Torah) was revealed by God. Like other good rabbis, Jesus made reference to God's law in his teaching. He would introduce a quotation or allusion to the Torah, saying, "You have heard that it was said ..." But then—and here's the shocking part—he would say, "But I say to you ...", to introduce his own interpretation of the law (see Mt 5:21–48).

Think about how this would sound from the Jewish perspective. Jesus refers to the divine Lawgiver, and then says, "But *I* say to you." As Pope Benedict XVI explained, "Jesus' 'I' is accorded a status that no teacher of the Law can legitimately allow himself."[1] Indeed, the crowds were "astonished"

---

[1] Joseph Ratzinger (Pope Benedict XVI), *Jesus of Nazareth*, vol. 1 (New York: Doubleday, 2007), 102.

by this teaching and recognized that Jesus was teaching with authority (Mt 7:28). He speaks with the authority of God, putting himself on par with the divine Lawgiver.

Jesus also asserted equality with God, saying, "I and the Father are one" (Jn 10:30). His claim to divinity was so clear to the Jewish leaders that they picked up stones to throw at him. They accused him of blasphemy, saying, "[Y]ou, being a man, make yourself God" (Jn 10:33). Similarly, one of the religious leaders in Jerusalem criticized Jesus, saying, "Are you greater than our father Abraham, who died? ... Who do you claim to be?" (Jn 8:53). Jesus responded with this most remarkable statement about his identity. He said, "Truly, truly, I say to you, before Abraham was, I am" (Jn 8:58).

Jesus makes two astonishing points here. First, he claims to have existed long before Abraham, the great father of faith who died some two thousand years before Jesus was born. No ordinary person would make such a claim! But Jesus goes even further. He says, "I am." "I am" (or, in Hebrew, "Yahweh") was God's holy name, which he revealed to Moses (see Ex 3:13). So holy is God's name in the Bible that no Jew would ever utter it. A first-century Jew hearing Jesus say, "Before Abraham was, I am", would understand Jesus to be alluding to the unutterable name of God and applying it to himself! Many of Jesus' hearers were appalled. They picked up stones to stone him to death for blasphemy (see Jn 8:58–59).

"Who Do You Say That I Am?"

What is most striking about Jesus' teaching is that he makes himself the central issue of faith. Other religious leaders in the world claimed to be a spiritual teacher or messenger sent from God. Buddha offered a spiritual way to find inner tranquility. Muhammad claimed to be Allah's prophet. Confucius taught moral principles to live a balanced life. But Jesus doesn't just offer a way to God or truth about God. He makes himself the essential issue of faith. He says, "*I am* the way, and the truth, and the life" (Jn 14:6; emphasis added). Similarly, he doesn't just call people to believe in God as other prophets and religious teachers throughout the centuries have done. He actually tells people to believe *in him*: "[H]e who believes has eternal life" (Jn 6:47).

What are we to do with a man who speaks and acts in the Person of God? For many, this Jesus who presents himself as the divine Lord is a bit unsettling. If Jesus is God, then he has authority over my life. If he really is who he claimed to be, then I must follow him. And that might mean making changes in the way I live. That's why many people prefer to view him as just a good moral teacher, someone who points us to God and even inspires us to be better people. We can contain that kind of Jesus. That Jesus remains far removed from our daily lives and doesn't entail our having to follow him. We can keep him at arm's reach, picking and choosing what we like about him, while setting aside those aspects that challenge us to grow and change.

But the real Jesus won't let us do that. The real Jesus challenges us to make a choice like no other religious leader does. Unlike Buddha, Muhammad, Confucius, or other religious founders, Jesus repeatedly acted and spoke as God. So he either is who he claimed to be or he's a very bad man, a liar who deceived millions of people throughout the world into thinking he was God. Or at best, he was a very confused man—someone who sincerely thought he was God but was not. We can accept Jesus as Lord, we can accuse him of being a liar, or we can feel sorry for him as a deluded extremist or crazy man. But, as C. S. Lewis pointed out, it does not make any sense to say Jesus was merely a good man, a wise moral teacher, and a spiritual guide. Jesus doesn't give us that option.[2]

The question Jesus asked his apostles two thousand years ago can be asked of us today: "Who do you say that I am?" (Mt 16:15). Will you accept him as who he claimed to be and welcome him as Lord of your life? That's a very personal question. But if you do welcome Jesus as the God who became man, then you are set to embark on the great journey of faith, an adventure of an intimate relationship with him.

Indeed, the entire Catholic faith centers on this fundamental question about Jesus. Who Jesus is shapes the way we understand love, morality, and justice. It shapes the way we live our friendships, marriages, and family lives. It sheds light on the important role of Mary and the saints, Peter and the papacy, and the Mass and the sacraments. It also sheds light on life after death: judgment, heaven, hell, and purgatory. And as we'll see next, Jesus stands at very center of human history and brings God's plan of salvation to its climax.

The Most Unexpected Way

I'll never forget the first time I knelt in the Church of the Holy Sepulcher in Jerusalem—the church built over the place where Jesus of Nazareth was crucified. The moment reinforces for me how *strange* Christianity really is.

On that day, I was just one of thousands of pilgrims who knelt there to pray and remember the death of a man who was crucified two thousand years earlier. I saw people from all over the world—Europe, Africa, Asia, North America, and South America—falling on their knees, bowing their

[2] C. S. Lewis, *Mere Christianity* (New York: Macmillan, 1960), pp. 55–56.

The Sea of Galilee, Israel

heads, folding their hands. Some were in tears, overwhelmed by the moment. Others were ecstatic, sharing their joy with their companions. Others silently took in the experience, closed their eyes, and whispered a short prayer. But what struck me most was how the many pilgrims that day joined literally *millions* of other Christians who throughout the centuries had traveled great distances and made tremendous sacrifices to come to this sacred ground and remember Jesus, the one who, we believe, reconciles us with the heavenly Father and rescues us from our suffering and sin.

But when we stop to think about it, we must admit that all this special attention given to Jesus is a bit strange to modern sensibilities. How is the death of a man two thousand years ago, in a city far away, relevant for my life? People today may be puzzled by the special reverence given to Jesus: Why should more attention be given to Jesus than to other spiritual leaders in the history of the world? Indeed, the Christian belief that God acted uniquely in one Person, in one city, at one particular time, in a way that has central importance for every person, is hard to grasp for many.

These are fair questions, but there are very good Jewish answers to these questions. And if we are to understand Jesus from within his original Jewish context, we must first grasp how the Jewish people saw their role in the story of God's plan for all humanity.

One Lord of All

The Jews believed that the one God who is over all nations had a special relationship with them. God loved the entire human family, but he began working with one particular people to gradually reveal himself and gather back his children in his saving plan. This one people of Israel would serve as God's instrument for reaching all the peoples of the earth. Hence, one could say that God chose Israel, not *instead of* the rest of the world, but *for the sake of* the rest of the world.

God's dramatic interactions with Israel, therefore, were always done with an eye to the rest of humanity. We can see this in three of the greatest gifts God entrusted to Israel: the *law* given at Mount Sinai, the *kingdom* dynasty given to David's family, and the *temple* in Jerusalem. These were given to Israel, not just for their sake, but so that the people eventually would share the blessings they had received with the nations, leading the peoples of the earth to the one true God.

We see this especially in the writings of Israel's prophets. After foreign powers destroyed Jerusalem, burned down the temple, and brought an end to the Davidic dynasty in 586 B.C., the prophets foretold that one day a new king would come to rescue the people from their enemies. He would restore the *kingdom* of Israel and draw all nations to worship the one true God (see Ps 2:8; 72:8–10, 17; 110:6).[3] It was believed that this king would be a new son of David, and he would come to the holy city of David, Jerusalem, to establish his reign. Some Jews in Jesus' day referred to this future king as the *messiah* (Hebrew for "anointed one"), for this son of David was expected to be the anointed king who would bring God's plan for Israel to fulfillment. Israel would become a "light to the nations" (Is 42:6; 49:6), God's *law* would go forth from Jerusalem to instruct all the peoples of the earth (see Is 2:2–4; Mic 4:1–5), and the *temple* in Jerusalem would become a house of prayer for all the nations (see Is 56:5–6; cf. Zech 14:17). God would come to rescue Israel, but in so doing, he would bring blessing to all humanity: one God, working with one particular people, to reunite all men and women into one covenant family.

It was into these hopes that Jesus stepped as he began his ministry with the Jewish people in the first century.

Putting the Pieces Together

Jesus Christ is the center of the whole Christian life, yet many of his followers today don't really know his story. They may have heard about the Sermon on the Mount, the Lord's Prayer, and the parable of the prodigal son. And they may know Jesus gathered disciples, healed the sick, and calmed a storm. But how do all of these different aspects of Christ's public ministry fit together? How do his various teachings, healings, miracles, prayers, exorcisms, and confrontations with his opponents fit into his overarching mission?

---

[3] See also Jer 23:5–8; 33:15–18; Ezek 37:21–28; Amos 9:11–12; Hag 2:21–22; Zech 3:8–10; 6:12–15.

Christians often focus on why Jesus died. And that, of course, is absolutely crucial. It's the climax of the story: Jesus died for our sins. But few consider another very important question: Why did Jesus *live*? If the only thing Jesus came to do was die, he could have done that as a baby when Herod tried to kill him (see Mt 2:12–18). Or he could have died at the start of his public life when people from his hometown tried to throw him over a cliff (see Lk 4:29). Jesus had these and other chances to die at the hands of his enemies, but he chose not to go to his death just yet. He had some important business to accomplish *with his life*, not just with his death.

And that important mission was the announcement of the kingdom of God. This was the central message of Christ's public ministry. It's what he talked about the most. As Jesus traveled from village to village for three years in Galilee, he constantly called people to repentance and proclaimed the gospel of the kingdom.

This is the central theme we will explore now as we walk step-by-step through the public ministry of Christ, from his baptism at the Jordan to his death on Calvary. This outline of Christ's life will help us better understand Jesus, his mission, and the Church he came to establish. And this foundation will shed much light on our Catholic faith, for everything we believe has roots in the Person and mission of Christ. To keep this simple, we will use one Gospel account as our main guide: the Gospel of Saint Matthew. If you'd like, you might even want to open your Bible and read along as we begin our walk through the life of Jesus.

The Baptism of Jesus (Mt 3)

Imagine the crisis the Jewish people were experiencing in the first century. For most of the last five hundred years,

God's people were oppressed by various foreign powers. Rome represented the latest and most powerful of regimes to afflict the people. Under Roman domination, taxation, and violence, the Jewish people were in many ways suffering as never before.

In the midst of this crisis, a strange figure appears in the desert, calling the people to "[r]epent"—to turn back to God—because "the kingdom of heaven is at hand" (Mt 3:2). The man's name is John, and he is preparing the people for the Lord who is coming to Israel to rescue his people.

John summons the Jews to be baptized in the Jordan River, a place charged with great symbolism. This was where Joshua many centuries ago led the Israelites, after forty years of journeying in the wilderness, to cross into the Promised Land at the culmination of the Exodus story. The prophets foretold that God would come to rescue his people from their enemies and restore the kingdom to Israel. And they sometimes depicted that restoration of Israel as a new exodus: just as God had liberated Israel from the Egyptians long ago, he would come again and free them from their new oppressors and reestablish his kingdom among them. So for John to announce that a new kingdom is dawning and to do so at the Jordan River would stir Jewish hopes about the royal son of David and God's coming to rescue the people in a new exodus. It's no wonder John's ministry drew so much attention and large crowds went out to follow him!

Then, one day, it finally happened. A young, unknown descendant of David from the obscure village of Nazareth visits John's movement in the desert. His name is Jesus, and he approaches John, asking for baptism. When Jesus comes out of the waters, the Spirit of God descends upon him, and a heavenly voice reveals his true identity: "This is my beloved Son, with whom I am well pleased" (Mt 3:17).

The Spirit's descent upon Jesus recalls how the Spirit came upon the kings of the Old Testament when they were anointed. One of the signs that Saul, for example, was truly the anointed king was that "the spirit of the LORD will come mightily upon [him]" (1 Sam 10:6). When David was anointed as king, "the Spirit of the LORD came mightily upon David from that day forward" (1 Sam 16:13). And the prophet Isaiah foretold that the future royal son of David would receive the Spirit upon him as a source of wisdom, understanding, counsel, and might (see Is 11:2). So when the Spirit comes upon Jesus at his baptism, this can be seen as a royal event, an anointing like the anointing of the kings of old. Indeed, when Jesus emerges from the waters with the Holy Spirit descending upon him, we have what the *Catechism* describes as "the manifestation ('Epiphany') of Jesus as Messiah of Israel and Son of God".[4]

The Temptations in the Desert (Mt 4)

Israel's kings were expected to fight the people's great battles. Saul battled the Philistines. David defeated Goliath. Josiah fought against the Egyptians. And the future messiah king would free the people from their enemies.

That's what makes Jesus' opening move so striking. After being anointed by the Spirit at the Jordan, Jesus doesn't begin his messianic mission by taking on the Roman oppressors. He instead goes out into the desert to confront a much fiercer opponent: the devil. And in so doing, he is making a very important point about his mission. The real enemy whom the Messiah confronts is not Herod, Pilate, or Caesar. The real enemy is the devil, the one who seduces all men into sin

[4] *CCC* 535; cf. Acts 10:38.

and leads people away from God. In this contest with Satan, Jesus enters the same three tests the Israelites faced in the desert when they first left Egypt in the Exodus—trials related to food, putting the Lord to the test, and idolatry—and he proves to be faithful precisely where Israel was unfaithful (see Ex 16:3; 17:3–18; 32:1–6). Jesus' initial triumph over Satan sets the tone for the rest of his public ministry. His proclaiming the kingdom of God, his healing people of their infirmities, and his forgiving people of their sins all can be seen as carrying out his victory over the devil in the lives of the people he meets, freeing them from the power and effects of sin. All this, of course, points to his climactic work on the cross, where Jesus definitively defeats the devil and brings salvation to the whole human family.

Proclamation of the Kingdom (Mt 5–7)

Jesus next launches his ministry in Galilee, gathering disciples and announcing a kingdom. Matthew's Gospel describes Jesus' public ministry as having two main pillars: preaching and healing. In fact, when Matthew sums up in one sentence what Jesus was doing in Galilee, he says, "[H]e went about all Galilee, ... *preaching* the gospel of the kingdom and *healing* every disease and every infirmity" (Mt 4:23; emphasis added; see Mt 9:35). Let's focus on the first pillar, Jesus' preaching.

The mere fact that Jesus was announcing a kingdom would stir many hopes. This is what the Jewish people were longing for: the coming of the king and the restoration of the kingdom. No wonder he immediately attracts people from all around the land! (See Mt 4:25.)

With this initial momentum, he leads his disciples up a mountain to give the core teaching of his kingdom in what has become known as the Sermon on the Mount. Just as

Mount Tabor, Israel

Moses went up a mountain and gave the people the law of the Old Covenant, so Jesus goes up a mountain to give the new law of the New Covenant he is establishing. But his vision for the kingdom in this sermon is not what most Jews were expecting. Far from a message of revolution, Jesus' teaching calls the people to a higher standard of love. Instead of rousing the people to fight off the gentile oppressors, Jesus calls the people to be peacemakers, to be merciful, and even to be willing to endure persecution (see Mt 5:1–48). He challenges them to go the extra mile for others, give alms to the poor, turn the other cheek, love their enemies, and pray for those who persecute them.

Such a message would have been surprising to many. Jesus is announcing a kingdom and gathering the people, but those who are peacemakers, who are merciful, who love their enemies, and who endure persecution were not the expected first-round draft picks for a kingdom-building team. Yet, Jesus is summoning the people to be what they were always meant to be: "light to the world" and "salt to the earth" (Mt 5:13–14). He reminds the people of their mission to the nations. The third promise to Abraham is about to be fulfilled. God's blessing is about to be poured out to all nations who will come to worship God, and that will be accomplished through the light of the faithful in Israel.

Healing Ministry (Mt 8–9)

It has been said that "actions speak louder than words". That expression is certainly true for the dramatic events following the Sermon on the Mount. In the great sermon, Jesus challenged the people to be light to the nations. Now, he puts his words into action as he touches a leper, cures a Roman centurion's servant, forgives people's sins, expels demons, gives sight to the blind, and eats meals with sinners and tax collectors. These were all people who, to varying degrees, were viewed as covenant outsiders, the unclean, those estranged from the mainstream life of first-century Judaism. Jesus' healings and interactions with these people fulfilled prophecy (see Is 29:18; 35:5–6), but they also sent a message about the kind of people he was gathering for his kingdom. By reaching out to the suffering, sinners, outcasts, and gentiles, Jesus embodies his message for Israel to be light to the world as he goes to all the dark corners of Israel, welcoming them into God's covenant family.

Foundations for the Kingdom (Mt 10–16)

As his movement grows, Jesus chooses twelve from among his many disciples to be leaders in his kingdom movement. These twelve men are known as the twelve apostles. The word "apostle" means "one who is sent", and these men are sent by Jesus to help carry out his mission in Israel. He vests them with his authority to do what he has been doing: preaching the gospel of the kingdom and healing the sick (see Mt 10:7). These are the men whom Jesus eventually will commission to proclaim his kingdom to the ends of the earth (see Mt 28:18–20).

The fact that Jesus chose *twelve* apostles is significant. This sacred number recalled the twelve tribes of Israel that descended from the twelve sons of the patriarch Jacob. By choosing twelve apostles, Jesus is making a powerful statement about his kingdom movement. He is signaling that God's plan to regather the tribes of Israel and restore the nation is now coming to fruition. A new Israel is emerging. Just as the nation was founded on the twelve sons of Jacob, the new Israel is centered on these twelve apostles of Jesus.

But among the twelve, there was one apostle who stood out: Simon Peter. Peter was the first person to confess explicitly that Jesus is the messiah. When Jesus asked the apostles, "Who do you say that I am?" it was Peter who responded, "You are the Christ, the Son of the living God" (Mt 16:15–16). What many people were hoping for, Peter was the first to state explicitly: Jesus is, indeed, the messiah. As a result, Jesus elevated Peter to serve as the head of the apostles, the rock upon which Christ would build his Church. And he gives Peter the symbolic "keys of the kingdom" (Mt 16:18–19), which in the Old Testament Scriptures signify the authority of one who runs the day-to-day affairs of the kingdom for a king (see Is 22:22). Peter is not the king, but he will play the important leadership role for Christ in his kingdom.

Journey to Jerusalem (Mt 16–20)

Once these foundations for his kingdom movement are laid in place—once Jesus establishes the apostles and Peter in their leadership roles—he suddenly starts talking about going to

Western Wall of the Temple, Jerusalem

Jerusalem, the city where the messiah was expected to establish his kingdom. Imagine the apostles' excitement over hearing that Jesus was the messiah and that he was now going to the royal city of David!

Then imagine their surprise when he told them he was going to Jerusalem, not to be enthroned in royal splendor like the kings of this world, but to die. *"From that time* Jesus began to show his disciples that he must go to Jerusalem and suffer many things from the elders and chief priests and scribes, and be killed, and on the third day be raised" (Mt 16:21; emphasis added).

Think of how shocking this must have been. That's not what the messiah was expected to do. The messiah was expected to triumph over his enemies and establish his kingdom in Jerusalem, not be killed there by his enemies!

Jesus was teaching an important lesson. All along his journey to Jerusalem, he spends much time reprogramming the apostle's understanding of the messiah's kingdom, which is not about worldly power and glory. When the apostles argue over who is going to be the greatest in the kingdom, Jesus says that the mark of true greatness in the kingdom is humility: "Whoever humbles himself like this child, he is the greatest in the kingdom of heaven" (Mt 18:4). When Peter asks how often they need to forgive, Jesus stresses that his kingdom is about persistent mercy, even forgiving people "seventy times seven" times (Mt 18:22). When the mother of two apostles asks Jesus for her sons to sit in the most honorable places in his kingdom, he emphasizes that his kingdom is about sacrificial service to others, "even as the Son of man came not to be served but to serve, and to give his life as a ransom for many" (Mt 20:28). His kingdom was about leaving everything else in this world aside to put Jesus first in one's life (see Mt 19:28–29). Ultimately, it was about his sacrificial love on the cross. Jesus foretold that he would be rejected by the elders and crucified (see Mt 16:21), and then he challenged his followers that if they want to be his disciples, they, too, must pick up the cross and follow him: "If any man would come after me, let him deny himself and take up his cross and follow me. For whoever would save his life will lose it, and whoever loses his life for my sake will find it" (Mt 16:24–25).

Jerusalem, the Temple, and Jesus (Mt 21–25)

Finally, Jesus enters the holy city of Jerusalem, and his first destination point is the temple. He's on a mission to address some urgent matters there, one of them being how the Jerusalem leaders turned the outer court of the temple—the place where the gentiles were supposed to worship—into a place of trade (see *CCC* 584). The prophet Isaiah proclaimed that the temple was to be "a house of prayer for all the nations" (Is 56:6–7), but Jesus was angered that it had become "a den of robbers" (Mt 21:13). Israel was supposed to be light to the world, but they were hindering the nations from coming to worship God in the holy city. He drove out the people selling animals for the temple sacrifices, and in this one swift, provocative action, he stopped the whole temple system for a while that day, preventing the temple from doing what it was supposed to do.

But this was just a foreshadowing of severer things to come. The temple sacrifices would soon cease forever. Later that same week, Jesus announced the destruction of the temple, of which there will not be left "one stone upon another" (Mt 24:2). Indeed, Jesus' prophecy came true: the temple was destroyed by the Romans in A.D. 70 and has never been rebuilt to this very day.

But for Jesus to march into Jerusalem, critique the temple leaders, bring a halt to the temple sacrifices, and announce the temple's impending destruction would have been quite alarming to many in the city, especially the chief priests, who were the custodians of the temple. They immediately begin plotting how to destroy him, and in just a few days, Jesus would pay the price.

The Triumph of the Cross (Mt 26–28)

Roman crucifixion was not just a form of execution. It was the way the Romans punished criminals with the maximum amount of pain and public humiliation. The person would be stripped and bound to a cross, with his arms extended and raised. The weight of the unsupported body would cause the breathing muscles to fatigue, causing a slow and painful death. The person eventually died of shock or asphyxiation, sometimes after the course of several days. The prisoner was raised up high and ridiculed by those passing by to show what happens to those who dare to resist Roman rule.

This background sheds light on how shocking it would have been for Jesus' followers to see their Lord be arrested by the chief priests and delivered to the Romans to be crucified. Many in Israel believed the messiah was coming to free the people from the Romans, not to be defeated by them in such a devastating way. A crucified messiah was not what people were expecting.

Yet, the Gospels show us there is more to the story. Jesus' death on Calvary was not his moment of defeat. It actually was his moment of triumph, as Israel's king.

One of the fascinating aspects of the Gospel accounts of Christ's death is how they depict his Crucifixion at the hands of the Romans as his royal triumph. In the middle of his trial, torture, and Crucifixion, a series of kingship images suddenly emerge just when we would least expect it. When the Roman governor Pilate interrogates Jesus, he focuses on one question: "Are you the *King* of the Jews?" (Mt 27:11; emphasis added). When Jesus is scourged by the Roman soldiers, the Gospels note how they dress him in "a *scarlet robe*", the color of royalty. They "put a *reed in his right hand*", symbolizing a royal staff, and put "a *crown* of thorns ... on his head". They then bow down and pay him homage, saying, "Hail, *King* of the Jews!" (Mt 27:28–29; emphasis added). When Jesus is crucified, a sign was put on the cross, reading, "This is Jesus the *King* of the Jews" (Mt 27:37; emphasis added). The chief priests at Calvary ridicule Jesus, saying, "He is the *King* of Israel; let him come down now from the cross" (Mt 27:42; emphasis added).

Clearly, the soldiers and chief priests employ all this royal imagery to mock Jesus. But the Gospels report these events to show how Jesus' executioners unwittingly reveal the truth about him: Jesus really is the king. And he establishes his kingdom with his death on the cross. Far from marking the failure of the messiah, Christ's death on Calvary is actually his enthronement. His death is not the moment of his defeat, but the moment of his victory over sin and the devil.

But how is this the case? How does the death of an innocent man solve the problem of our sin? That's the topic of our next chapter.

Chapter Five

The Triumph of the Cross

The earliest surviving depiction of Christ's Crucifixion was found carved on a wall near the Palatine Hill in Rome. It likely goes back to the year A.D. 200 but challenges us today to consider how strange and unexpected Christ's death on the cross really was. And what's fascinating about this depiction is that it was forged not by a Christian but by a Roman who was mocking the Christian worship of a crucified God.

The shocking graffiti-styled image portrays Christ on a cross having the head of a donkey. And below the cross stands a Christian named Alexamenos. The graffiti inscription ridicules the Christian by saying, "Alexamenos worships his God."

This mocking of Christian belief is somewhat understandable. For the Romans, crucifixion was the most horrible and shameful way to die. The Roman orator Cicero once said, "The very word 'cross' should be far removed not only from the person of a Roman citizen but from his thoughts, his eyes and his ears."[1] So when the early Christians proclaimed their belief in the crucified Christ, the gospel message seemed appalling to many in pagan Rome.

Why do Christians worship a crucified God? Why did God become man and die for our sins on a cross? Couldn't

[1] Cicero, "In Defense of Rabirius", 16, in *The Speeches of Cicero*, trans. H. Gross Hodge (Cambridge, Mass.: Harvard, 1952), p. 467.

there have been another way to save humanity from its sins? These are some of the questions we will explore as we consider the mystery of Christ's death and Resurrection.

"Why Have You Forsaken Me?"

Picture the scene on Good Friday. Jesus was abandoned by most of his disciples, rejected by the people he came to save, and sentenced to the most horrific kind of execution known in the Roman Empire: crucifixion.

At first glance, Jesus' death on the cross seems to be his moment of defeat, a great tragedy, the end of his mission. And in his dying moments, in his agony on the cross, he cries out, "My God, my God, why have you forsaken me?" (Mk 15:34).

What do these mysterious words mean? Was Jesus completely abandoned by his Father on the cross? These words would have been familiar to a Jew of the first century, for they come from the Jewish Scriptures. Jesus is reciting the first words of Psalm 22. The psalm expresses the prayer of a righteous man who is suffering greatly at the hands of his enemies. He is pushed to the extreme limits of grief and experiences unendurable suffering, to the extent that he feels as if he has been abandoned by God. "My God, my God, why have you forsaken me?" (Ps 22:1).

The righteous man goes on to tell how his enemies have "pierced [his] hands and feet" (Ps 22:16), divided his garments among them, and for his raiment they cast lots (see Ps 22:18). They mock him, saying, "He committed his cause to the LORD; let him deliver him" (Ps 22:8).

This is exactly what happens to Jesus on Good Friday. Psalm 22 prophetically foreshadows Christ's suffering on the cross, for like the suffering man in this psalm, Jesus also will

Alexamenos Graffiti, Museo Nazionale, Rome

have his hands and feet pierced when he's crucified; his garments will be divided; and the soldiers will cast lots for them (see Mt 27:35), while the chief priests and elders mock Jesus saying, "He trusts in God; let God deliver him now" (Mt 27:43).

But that's not the end of the story. The psalm goes on to describe how even in the midst of this darkness, God's righteous servant clings to the Lord in hope, trusting that the God of Israel will save him. He even sees that his suffering will somehow play a part in God's plan of salvation, helping extend God's reign over all the earth. The psalm reaches its climax with these triumphant words: "All the ends of the earth shall remember and turn to the LORD; and all the families of the nations shall worship before him. For dominion belongs to the LORD, and he rules over the nations" (Ps 22:27–28).

So Jesus' cry from the cross, far from being a cry of despair, is actually a prayer of hope in the face of great darkness. Christ didn't experience reprobation as if he himself had sinned. Rather, his love drove him to unite himself with us sinners, to the extent that he could say in our name, "My God, my God, why have you forsaken me?" (see *CCC* 603). At the same time, his prayer from the cross points to the profound union the Son maintains with the Father even in the midst of this terrible darkness. Jesus quotes Psalm 22 and, in so doing, shows his trust in the Father that even this darkest hour of his Crucifixion was all a part of the Father's plan to bring his kingdom and salvation to the whole world.

The Passover Lamb

Psalm 22 is just one of many biblical passages that point to different aspects of the mystery of Christ's death. The many sacrifices of the Jewish temple, for example, point to the ultimate sacrifice of Christ that takes away all sin. Abraham's offering of his son Isaac on Mount Moriah foreshadows the heavenly Father giving up his only beloved Son Jesus, who will be sacrificed in the same place (see Gen 22). The suffering servant of the Lord whom Isaiah foretold would be "wounded for our transgressions", bear "the sin of many", pour out "his soul to death", and make himself "an offering for sin" (Is 53:5, 12, 10) also anticipates the Savior's sacrifice on Calvary.

But the biblical theme that seems to be at the forefront of Jesus' mind in the hours leading up to his Passion and death was the Passover. The night before he died, Jesus celebrated the Passover meal with his apostles. On this most holy of Jewish feasts, the people retold and reenacted the first Passover, that fateful night when God liberated the people from slavery in Egypt. On that night, God instructed the

Israelites to slay an unblemished lamb, eat of its flesh, and then mark their doorposts with the lamb's blood (see Ex 12:1–27). Those who celebrated this feast would be spared the punishment that was to fall on everyone else in Egypt. The Egyptian firstborn were struck down that night while God passed over the homes that had the lamb's blood marking them. After this most severe of all the plagues to afflict Egypt, Pharaoh finally released the people from slavery that very night.

Each year after that, the Israelites remembered this founding event of their nation's history by celebrating the Passover. They would sacrifice a lamb and eat it in a sacred meal to express their solidarity with their ancestors who escaped Egypt in the first Passover. It was that meal which Jesus celebrated shortly before he died, a meal known as the Last Supper.

But what's striking about the New Testament accounts of the Last Supper is that there is no mention of the lamb. The lamb was the main course, the climax, of the Passover feast. Yet, just when we might expect to hear about the Passover lamb, Jesus did something surprising.

> Jesus took bread, and blessed, and broke it, and gave it to the disciples and said, "Take, eat; this is my body." And he took a chalice, and when he had given thanks he gave it to them, saying, "Drink of it, all of you; for this is my blood of the covenant, which is poured out for many for the forgiveness of sins". (Mt 26:26–28)

Notice how instead of mentioning the lamb that was normally offered up in the Passover sacrifice, Jesus speaks about his own body being offered up. And instead of the lamb's sacrificial blood being mentioned, Jesus speaks of his own blood being poured out in sacrifice. Jesus identifies himself with the Passover lamb! It's *his* body that will be offered up, and *his* blood that will poured out in sacrifice on Calvary.

Church of the Holy Sepulcher, Jerusalem

Jesus viewed his own death on the cross, not merely as an execution, but as a new kind of Passover sacrifice. Just as the Passover lamb was sacrificed to spare the firstborn in Egypt, so Jesus is sacrificed on the cross to spare all of humanity.

How the Cross Works

Still, we must ask how Jesus' death on the cross brings about the salvation of the world. One popular interpretation emphasizes Christ as the innocent victim who voluntarily stepped in to take our punishment. We deserved death, but Jesus offered to take the full brunt of the divine wrath that we sinners deserved. In this perspective, Jesus receives the punishment for sin instead of us, so that we can now enter the kingdom of heaven.

The Catholic tradition, however, sees that the reconciling power of the cross is centered not simply on his enduring punishment but most of all in his offering of love. Jesus lovingly makes himself an offering for our sin, bearing our iniquities, and substituting his obedience to the Father for our disobedience. But, it's the magnitude of Christ's love that pleases God, not the amount of suffering he experienced. After all, how could God the Father be pleased with the tortuous killing of his innocent Son?

Imagine if a child disobeyed his father and was going to receive a spanking for his punishment. At the last minute, however, the child's older brother volunteers to take the spanking instead. The father says he doesn't care whom he punishes. He just needs to fulfill justice and pour out his wrath on someone for the disobedience. So he spanks the volunteering older brother and forgives the younger one. How does *that* possibly bring about a loving reconciliation between father and son?

A God who punishes the innocent instead of the guilty would not be merciful or just. He would be completely arbitrary. As Saint John Paul II explained, what gives the Cross its "redemptive value is not the material fact that an innocent person has suffered the chastisement deserved by the guilty and that justice has thus been in some way satisfied." Rather, the saving power of the Cross "comes from the fact that the innocent Jesus, out of pure love, entered into solidarity with the guilty and thus transformed their situation from within."[2] In other words, what makes Christ's death on Calvary redemptive is not the fact that punishment has been meted out on an innocent victim or that God's anger has been appeased. Rather, what gives Christ's work on Calvary its saving power is his unique and total gift of himself in love.

[2]John Paul II, "General Audience", October 26, 1988, in *Jesus, Son and Savior: A Catechesis on the Creed* (Boston: Pauline Books and Media, 1996), 445.

As the *Catechism* states, "It is love 'to the end' (Jn 13:1) that confers on Christ's sacrifice its value as redemption and reparation, as atonement and satisfaction" (*CCC* 616).

The Cross of Love

The cross reveals Christ's saving love in two main ways. First, it underscores the depths to which Jesus descended to save us from sin. Even though we sinned, the divine Son of God sought us out and identified himself with sinful humanity. He entered our world, became one of us, and even experienced the effects of our sin, which include alienation, suffering, and death. Throughout his public ministry, Jesus consistently went out to the darkest corners of Israel to meet people precisely where suffering and the powers of evil flourished the most. He touched the untouchable lepers and cured the blind and the lame. He shared meals in fellowship with some of the most notorious sinners. And he even approached people who had been possessed by demons. At every step of the way, Jesus went out to the sinners and outcasts, calling them to repentance, and through his solidarity with them, he restored them to covenant union with God.

This all reaches its culmination on the cross. There, Jesus plunged into the depths of humanity's suffering, experiencing the curse that has plagued us ever since the fall: death. He who was without sin "could take upon himself that which is the effect of sin, namely, suffering and death, giving to the sacrifice of his life a real value and a perfect redemptive meaning."[3] In uniting himself so fully to the human family, which had been estranged from God and suffering under the

[3] Ibid., 445.

curse of death, Jesus could lift us out of the grave with him in his Resurrection and restore us to unity with the Father.

Jesus could do this because, secondly, he offered the one perfect gift of love that could reconcile us with God: his sacrificial death on Calvary. A key point to understand here is how sin ruptures our relationship with God. All sin, in the end, is an offense against the all-good and all-holy God. It is a rejection of his infinite love for us and separates us from him.

Our relationship with God, like all human relationships, needs to be repaired if it becomes broken because of sin. In a marriage, for example, if a husband has hurt his wife and he wants to repair the relationship, he will do something to make amends, to bring about reconciliation, to make up for his lack of love. He, of course, will say, "I'm sorry." But he senses he should do something more. He might give her an embrace, buy her flowers, or take her out to dinner. He might make a sacrifice for her or perform some kind deed for her—some meaningful act of love that overshadows the lack of love he showed her. And the magnitude of that gift of love will correspond to the seriousness of the hurt he inflicted on the relationship.

The same is true in our relationship with God. Our sin entails withholding our love for the God who so completely loves us. We, therefore, should offer God a gift of love that corresponds to the infinite gravity of sin committed against him. But no human being can do that. Not even the most saintly person could offer a gift of love that would atone for the sins of all humanity. Only a divine person could do that.

This is why the Son of God became man in Jesus Christ.[4] As the God-Man, Jesus alone reconciles us to the Father. Being

[4] "Now a mere man could not have satisfied for the whole human race, and God was not bound to satisfy; hence it behooved Jesus Christ to be both God and man" (St. Thomas Aquinas, *Summa Theologica* III, q. 1, art. 2).

truly human, Jesus can represent humanity and offer an act of love on our behalf. But because Jesus is fully divine, his act of love on the cross has a value that far surpasses anything a mere human being could offer to God. If you or I died on a cross, it would not bring salvation to the world. No mere finite person could ever offer such a gift. But because of who Jesus is—fully human and fully divine—his act of total, self-giving love on the cross takes on infinite value. In fact, as Saint Bernard of Clairvaux is often attributed as saying, "The smallest drop of Christ's blood would have been enough to have redeemed all mankind."[5] Jesus offers the one supreme act of sacrificial self-giving that can reconcile us to the Father.

The Third Day

One of the most intriguing aspects of Christianity is the fact that it got started at all.

Around Jesus' time, there were a dozen or so other Jewish leaders claiming to be messiahs or prophets who quickly came in and out. They started movements, rallied the people, and claimed that God would work through them to bring about his kingdom. In each case they were killed by the pagan enemy.

When Jesus was a boy, a Jewish man named Judas the Galilean, for example, led a tax revolt against Rome, and he and hundreds of his followers were captured and crucified. In A.D. 66 another revolutionary named Simon bar Giora led Jerusalem in its war against the Roman armies before surrendering and being sent to Rome, where he was paraded through the streets and executed in the Roman forum. And about one

---

[5] See Aquinas, *Questiones quodlibertales* II, q. 1, a. 2. See also Paul Murray, *Aquinas at Prayer: The Bible, Mysticism and Poetry* (London: Bloomsbury, 2013), 253.

Golgotha Shrine, Church of the Holy Sepulcher, Jerusalem

From the *Symbolon* series

hundred years after Jesus' death, another leader named Simon ben Kosiba was hailed by leading rabbis as the people's messiah before being captured by the Romans and killed.

In every instance, when the leader died, their movements either died with them or were changed into another movement based on a new messianic leader. The pattern is clear: if you follow a messiah who is killed by the Romans, it must not have been the true messiah you were following. It's time to put your hope in someone else. That's what happened in every case—except with Jesus.

Like the others, Jesus started a messianic movement and was crucified by the Romans. But when he died, his movement didn't die. It actually grew exponentially. And Jesus' followers didn't turn to someone else—a relative or disciple of Jesus—to serve as the new messiah figure. Surprisingly, they went on proclaiming the crucified Jesus as messiah. How strange! A movement centered on a crucified man as Lord and King would not be appealing to most in the ancient world. As Saint Paul admits, the whole idea of the cross seems crazy to the world. It's a "stumbling block to Jews" and "folly to gentiles" (1 Cor 1:23). Still, Paul refers to the crucified Jesus as "Christ", which is the Greek expression for "messiah", well over one hundred times in his writings. And the apostles and other early followers of Jesus went all over the world and even to their deaths proclaiming that the Jesus who was killed by the Romans is the true messiah, and they somehow inspired countless people to accept this crucified messiah as Lord.

How do we account for a messianic movement like this? Insights from New Testament scholar N. T. Wright challenge us to ask two questions: First, why didn't Christ's followers either give up or pin their hopes on another messiah figure?[6] That's what everyone else did when their leader died. What made Jesus' death different from that of all the other would-be messiahs? Second, how could Jesus' followers convincingly proclaim a *crucified* messiah? The messiah was expected by many to liberate the Jewish people from the Roman enemy. No one was looking for a messiah who would be executed by the Romans. How, therefore, could the early Christians proclaim that the crucified Jesus was actually the long-awaited messiah king?

The early Christians gave one consistent answer to these questions: because after Jesus was crucified, died, and was buried, God raised him from the dead.

Over the centuries, and especially in modern times, skeptics have tried to manage the mystery of Easter morning in a

[6] N. T. Wright *The Resurrection of the Son of God* (Minneapolis: Fortress Press, 2003), especially pp. 685–738. See also N. T. Wright, "The Transforming Reality of Bodily Resurrection" in Marcus Borg and N. T. Wright, *The Meaning of Jesus: Two Visions* (New York: HarperCollins, 1999), 111–27.

way that avoids the Christian belief that Jesus rose again from the dead. Some, for example, have proposed that perhaps Jesus never actually died on Good Friday but survived the trauma of the Crucifixion and was seen alive sometime later. Others have speculated that maybe the first witnesses went to the wrong tomb and, finding it empty, mistakenly concluded that Jesus came back to life. Still others have theorized that Jesus' disciples were so overwhelmed by grief at his passing that they imagined seeing him alive and well, not realizing they were experiencing hallucinations. Most of these "alternative explanations" are far from convincing and need not claim our serious attention. However, there are two others you may have encountered and wondered about.

Some both in ancient and modern times have tried to discredit early Christian testimony to Jesus' Resurrection by saying the apostles stole the body from the tomb and made up the story about Jesus being alive again. Such a hypothesis, however, seems quite unlikely since there was a large stone covering the entrance of the tomb and there were Roman soldiers guarding it. It doesn't seem likely that the apostles could have pulled this off. Think about how they abandoned Jesus on Good Friday and were hiding behind closed doors "for fear of the Jews" (Jn 20:19), so afraid that they might be arrested for their association with Christ. Is it likely that these men would suddenly muster up the courage and risk their lives to take on the Roman soldiers, move the massive stone, and steal the body?

Others today try to explain away belief in the Resurrection of Jesus, saying Jesus is risen from the dead, but only in a metaphorical sense. In this perspective, the Resurrection was a myth, a metaphor for Christ's triumph over evil, a sign of how Jesus remains with us spiritually, or a symbol of how Christ's story is still meaningful for us today. Jesus rose "spiritually" and remains alive in our hearts. But as Father Robert Barron put it,

From the *Symbolon* series

Resurrection of Jesus, Basilica of St. John Lateran, Rome

"This kind of speculation is born in faculty lounges, for few in the first century would have found that kind of talk the least bit convincing." He goes on: "Can you imagine Paul tearing into Corinth or Athens or Philippi with the message that there was an inspiring dead man who symbolized the presence of God? No one would have taken him seriously."[7] Rather, it was the conviction that Jesus did something no one else had ever done before—the conviction that Jesus rose from the dead—that drove his early followers to the ends of the earth and even to their deaths proclaiming Jesus as Lord.

More Than Good Friday

When it comes to answering the question about how we are saved, many Christians focus only on Jesus' death. Jesus paid the price and died on the cross for our sins. But the Bible

[7] Fr. Robert Barron, *Catholicism* (New York: Image Books, 2011), 85.

and the Catholic Church emphasize the importance of the entire mystery of Christ: the Son of God becoming man and Christ's life, death, and descent to the dead, as well as his Resurrection, Ascension, and sending of the Holy Spirit at Pentecost. Let's step back and consider more of what happened after Jesus died, walking with him from his descent to the dead on Holy Saturday to his Ascension into heaven forty-one days later (the descent of the Holy Spirit will be discussed in the next chapter).

Descent to the Dead (Holy Saturday)

In the Creed, we make an intriguing statement about what happened after Jesus died. We proclaim, "He descended into hell." What does this mysterious statement mean? Like all men who had experienced death, Jesus' soul descended to the realm of the dead. This place was sometimes called "hell" (*sheol* in Hebrew or *hades* in Greek), because souls there could not see God face-to-face. The gates of heaven were not yet opened to the holy souls who awaited their Savior. Jesus descended to the dead, not to liberate the damned (see *CCC* 633), but to complete his messianic mission and bring redemption to the just who had gone before him, to "the dead [who] will hear the voice of the Son of God, and those who hear will live" (Jn 5:25). It is this announcement of the good news to the dead that we commemorate on the day known as "Holy Saturday", the day after Good Friday. We also see in Jesus' descent into hell the fullness of Christ's saving work in that Jesus even redeems death. When Jesus assumed a human nature, he healed and redeemed every aspect of what it means to be human. In his descent to the dead, Jesus experiences human death in a complete and real way, but at the same time, he redeems death, causing it to become the birth into fullness of life in Christ. This is why Jesus' Resurrection from the dead is the cornerstone of the Christian faith—because not even death can separate us from the love of Christ.

The Resurrection (Easter Sunday)

The Resurrection of Jesus is not a return to earthly life. People in the Gospels such as Lazarus or Jairus' daughter were raised from the dead. They return to earthly life, but they will die again some day. Jesus' Resurrection is different. "In his risen body he passes from the state of death to another life beyond time and space" (*CCC* 646). Christ's humanity enters the glory of God and is taken into the life of the Trinity. His body now belongs to the realm of his heavenly Father. This is why the Gospel accounts report Jesus appearing whenever and however he wills. He can pass through walls to his apostles, appear to Mary Magdalene as a gardener, and appear as a stranger to his disciples on the road to Emmaus. The risen Jesus shows the apostles on Easter that his resurrected body is the same body that was crucified on Good Friday: they can touch the wounds in his hands, feet, and side. But his body is also different. It's now glorified, taking on new characteristics. It is not limited to time and space.

His humanity entering the realm of his Father is an essential part of our redemption. To save us, Jesus did more than die for our sins. He also rose to give us new life. As Saint Augustine once said, "The dead Christ would be of no benefit to us unless he had risen from the dead."[8] Similarly, Saint

---

[8] St. Augustine, *Sermo* 246, 2 (*PL* 38, 1154), in *The Mystery of Jesus Christ* (Dublin: Four Courts Press, 1994), 164.

Paul highlights how Jesus "was put to death for our trespasses and *raised for our justification*" (Rom 4:25; emphasis added). The Son of God who became man and experienced the effects of sin—namely, suffering and death—now rises from the dead, and his humanity enters the glory of God. This opens the pathway for us to new life in him. The life of the Son of God can now dwell in us as we become God's adopted children through grace (as we'll see in the next chapter). His Resurrection also is the source of our future resurrections. Jesus is "the first fruits of those who have fallen asleep", and all who share in Christ's life will rise with him on the last day (1 Cor 15:20–22).

The Ascension (Ascension Thursday)

After remaining with the apostles for forty days after Easter, teaching them about the kingdom of God, Jesus ascended into heaven, where he is seated at the right hand of the Father. This marks the definitive entry of Christ's humanity "into divine glory" (*CCC* 659).

In the Bible, the right hand is the position of authority. The One who exists as the divine Son of God for all ages is glorious and all-powerful for all ages. But now, after he took on human flesh and his body was glorified, he is seated bodily at the right hand of God. In this exalted position, Jesus prepares a place for us in his Father's realm, constantly intercedes for us, and reigns over heaven and earth in his kingdom that will have no end. And it was from the right hand of the Father that Jesus sent the Holy Spirit on Pentecost.

Chapter Six

"Clothed with Power from On High"

The Holy Spirit and the Life of Grace

Forty days after the Resurrection, Jesus meets with his apostles one last time before ascending into heaven. He wants to tell them about a profound gift they will soon receive. He instructs them to remain in Jerusalem until they are "clothed with power from on high" (Lk 24:49).

Jesus is referring here to the gift of the Holy Spirit, a gift to which the Jewish Scriptures had alluded long before. The prophets foretold that one day God would send his Spirit into our hearts to give us new life, enabling us to do what we could not do on our own. The Spirit would cleanse us of sin, transform our hard hearts, and empower us to walk in God's ways (see Ezek 36:25–27; 37:14). Jesus himself had alluded to this when he promised the apostles that the Father would send the Holy Spirit to dwell within them, to teach them all things, guide them in truth, and take all that is Christ's and give it to them (see Jn 14:15, 25–26).

Now the moment is here. In his last words to the apostles before ascending to heaven, Jesus tells them to get ready for the long-awaited outpouring of God's Spirit. The disciples gathered for nine days of prayer in Jerusalem to prepare themselves for this powerful gift, and then it happened:

*Descent of the Holy Spirit (detail in Holy Door at
St. Paul Outside the Walls, Rome)*

And suddenly a sound came from heaven like the rush of
a mighty wind, and it filled all the house where they were
sitting. And there appeared to them tongues as of fire, dis-
tributed and resting on each one of them. And they were
all filled with the Holy Spirit and began to speak in other
tongues, as the Spirit gave them utterance. (Acts 2:2–4)

Consider all that happens to the apostles next. These men are
dramatically changed. On Good Friday, almost all of them ran
away and abandoned Jesus on the cross. They were scared,
hiding, and afraid that they would be arrested next. But now,
on this day known as Pentecost, these same men are "clothed
with power from on high". They are filled with the Holy
Spirit and exhibit great courage and zeal. They boldly proclaim Jesus Christ is Israel's messiah risen from the dead, and

as a result, three thousand are converted and baptized that very day. And from this point forward, the apostles are driven to the ends of the earth, announcing the gospel and giving witness to Christ no matter what the cost, willing even to go to their deaths in the footsteps of their Lord.

This transformation that the Holy Spirit accomplished in the apostles is the kind of change he wants to work in all of us. It may not happen as dramatically and as rapidly for everyone, but God wants to meet us in our sins, fears, weaknesses, and failures and fill us with his Holy Spirit to change us into Christ's likeness "from one degree of glory to another" (2 Cor 3:18). He wants us to be "clothed with power from on high" so that we can be transformed into the saintly men and women we're called to be.

Who Is the Holy Spirit?

The average Christian might have a picture in his mind of God the Father or of Jesus, God the Son. But the Holy Spirit seems more mysterious. The Bible uses various images to depict the Spirit: he is associated with the image of a dove descending on Jesus at his baptism, the cloud guiding Israel in the desert, or the fire descending on the apostles at Pentecost (see Mt 3:16; Ex 13:21; Acts 2:3).

But who exactly is the Holy Spirit? And what does the Holy Spirit do in our lives?

The Holy Spirit is the third Person of the Holy Trinity, the bond of love between the Father and the Son. And the God who is love gives us his own love as his first and greatest gift. He accomplishes this through the sending of the Spirit: "God's love has been poured into our hearts through the Holy Spirit who has been given to us" (Rom 5:5).

At baptism, the Holy Spirit takes up residence in us and brings us into communion with God. Think about how amazing this is: God's own Spirit dwells within us! This brings all kinds of effects in the soul: the Spirit forgives our sins and breathes God's love into us. This life in the Spirit transforms us, healing us of our weaknesses and empowering us to live like Christ. The Spirit prompts us, guides us, and enables us to bear witness to Christ in the world. The Spirit does all this by infusing us with a gift that the Church calls "sanctifying grace"—a grace that sanctifies (which means "to make holy").

Amazing Grace

Here, we need to step back and consider the amazing work the Spirit performs in our souls through grace. Christians often talk about grace, but few understand what it actually is. Grace is the free gift of God's divine life in us. Through sanctifying grace, we are not just forgiven and healed of sin. We become children of God, adoptive sons and daughters, sharing in God's own life (see *CCC* 1996–97).

Now it is absolutely crucial to understand the Catholic realism of this. This idea of sharing in God's life and becoming his children is not mere metaphor or pious talk. God became man not just to free us from sin, but to make us his sons and daughters in Christ Jesus, the Son of God himself, *sharing in his divinity.*

This is a point the New Testament makes in the Second Letter of Peter: we actually become "partakers of the divine nature" (2 Pet 1:4). God really invites us to participate in his divine life, and this sharing in Christ's life transforms us and makes us children of God in Christ, the Son of God himself. We thus become children of God, not just in name, but in reality. Saint John marvels over this gift: "See what love the Father has given us, that we should be called children of God; *and so we are....* Beloved, we are God's children now" (1 Jn 3:1–2; emphasis added).

Notice, Saint John did not say we are just *called* God's children. We are called God's children because that is *what we really are.* In other words, because Christ's Spirit really dwells in our hearts, because the divine life of the Son of God is in us, we truly have God as our Father. We become, to use a classical expression, "sons in the Son". As Saint Paul said, "[B]ecause you are sons, God has sent the Spirit of his Son into our hearts, crying, 'Abba! Father!' " (Gal 4:6).

Iron in Fire

Several of the Church Fathers explained that this real sharing in Christ's divine sonship is the main reason God became man: the Son of God became the son of man so that the sons of men might become sons of God. Saint Athanasius put it most dramatically: "For the Son of God became man so that we might become God."[1]

This, of course, doesn't mean that we become God himself or that we become junior deities. We remain human beings. But through God's grace, our human nature is elevated to participate in God's divine nature. We are able to live "supernaturally", meaning above and beyond what our human nature could do on its own.

One analogy from the tradition can be helpful here. When an iron rod is put into a flame of fire, it begins to change

---

[1] *CCC* 460, quoting St. Athanasius, *On the Incarnation*, 54, 3: *PG* 25, 192B.

From the *Symbolon* series

"Dove Window" (part of Throne of St. Peter by Bernini),
St. Peter's Basilica, Vatican City

and take on the properties of fire. It becomes hot. It starts to glow, taking on the color of the fire. And it emits smoke, like the fire itself. The rod of iron doesn't become fire. But it takes on the characteristics of fire.

Similarly, when our human nature is infused with sanctifying grace through the fire of the Holy Spirit, it starts to change. It is gradually transformed by God so that it begins to take on the characteristics of Christ himself. The soul exhibits more peace, joy, patience, generosity, and love. The soul does not become God, but takes on more of the characteristics of God as it is being transformed by the fire of his love.

Let's think about what this really means. In what way do we take on the characteristics of the Son of God? The life of the Son of God is all about total, self-giving love. Within the Holy Trinity, the Son of God, for all eternity, gives himself completely in love to the Father. All that he is, he pours out in love to the Father, holding nothing back. And when the Son of God became man in Jesus, he did the same thing. He continued to give himself completely in love to the Father, culminating on Calvary where he poured himself out even unto death, death on a cross.

It is this total, self-giving love of the Son of God that we participate in through grace. Through his grace, Christ, in a sense, reproduces his life in us, enabling us to live like he does in complete, sacrificial love. The more we cooperate with this grace, the more we as sons of God begin to see as he sees, act as he acts, and love as he loves. The more Christ's love works through us, the more we can say with Saint Paul, "[I]t is no longer I who live, but Christ who lives in me" (Gal 2:20). Through sanctifying grace, the Holy Spirit bears such fruit in our lives. This is why grace is truly, as the traditional hymn says, "amazing"!

The Law Written on Our Hearts

When God, in the Old Testament book of Jeremiah, foretold of the New Covenant, he spoke of the great work he would do in our hearts. He contrasts the old law he gave the Israelites on Mount Sinai with the new law he will give the world in the future.

In the Old Testament, the Ten Commandments were written on tablets of stone and given to Moses on Mount Sinai. But even though the people knew the law, they did not live it out. They were explicitly told what is right and wrong, but their hearts were weak and they did not have the power to follow God's plan. It's as if they were given the instruction manual, but the batteries were not included.

The new law, however, would not just be an external command. God foretold how it would be something *interior*. "I will put my law within them, and I will write it upon their hearts" (Jer 31:33). The new law would give people power in their souls to walk faithfully in God's ways.

This new law is revealed by Christ and calls us to be perfect as our heavenly Father is perfect and to love as Christ loves. But it is not just a high ethical ideal. The most profound aspect of the new law is that it involves the inner work of the Holy Spirit, which makes it possible for us to live like Christ. Jesus doesn't just reveal the vision for the new law in the Sermon on the Mount; he also sends his Spirit through the sacraments to give us the grace to live it (see *CCC* 1965–66). Indeed, the Holy Spirit is the divine Lawgiver himself dwelling in the depths of the human heart, prompting us, inspiring us, and guiding us to live like Christ.

One of the main ways God writes his law in our hearts is through what are called the gifts of the Holy Spirit.

Gifts and Fruits of the Spirit

When we're baptized, we receive the gifts of the Holy Spirit, which are dispositions that make us docile to God's promptings. God wants to guide us, inspire us, and lead us in our daily lives so that we live according to the Spirit, which is the way of Christ's love. And he steers us away from living according the flesh, which is the way of self-love. These gifts of the Spirit—wisdom, understanding, counsel, fortitude,

Guiding Star Pilgrimmages, LLC

Church of the Visitation, interior. Ein Karem, Israel

knowledge, piety, and fear of the Lord—help us to notice those moments when God knocks on the door of our hearts. They help us to respond in generosity when God nudges us and invites us to give more of ourselves to him and to the people in our lives.

This does not involve anything spiritually extraordinary, such as hearing voices or having visions. We may sometimes simply sense God wants us to visit a friend, ask someone's forgiveness, or take more time with our spouse or a particular child. We might sense we should stop by the chapel to pray, make a small sacrifice, not respond to a situation in anger, or endure a difficulty with more cheerfulness. These simple movements of the Spirit happen all the time in ordinary, prayerful Christians, and the gifts of the Holy Spirit help us to follow those divine promptings more faithfully.

Here we are touching upon the real drama of the Christian life: allowing the Holy Spirit to sanctify us—make us holy—by becoming ever more docile to his workings in our hearts. Every day, God gives us opportunities to grow in kindness, patience, humility, and trust. Every day, the Holy Spirit invites us to live more for others and not for self, to live according to the Spirit and not according to the flesh. The more we cooperate with the Holy Spirit's inspirations, the more we live like Christ and mature as God's sons and daughters.

We should, therefore, ask the Holy Spirit for his guidance each day. We should beg God, "Inspire me in all my actions. Guide me in all my decisions"—whether it be in our families, our workplaces, our parishes, or our communities. And then we should endeavor to be faithful to those promptings—to those opportunities, both small and big, that God gives us to show our love for him: to serve more, to give more, to trust more, to love more.

The more we live according to the Spirit and less according to the flesh, the more the Spirit bears fruit in our lives. We are gradually being changed, becoming more like Christ. We exhibit greater joy, peace, patience, kindness, purity, and self-control. With these and other fruits of the Spirit evident in our lives, we bring a blessing to those around us and become a more powerful witness to Christ in the world (see *CCC* 1832; Gal 5:22–23).

The Dove Window

In the Creed, Christians say that the Holy Spirit is "the Lord and the giver of life". We've seen the various ways the Spirit works in us and fills us with God's life. And he does this through the life of the Church. Whether it be through the inspired Scriptures, Sacred Tradition, and the Magisterium, or the sacraments, the lives of the saints, or the Church at prayer, the Holy Spirit animates the Church by bringing souls into deeper communion with God.

This point can be illustrated by the architecture inside of St. Peter's Basilica in Rome.

Behind the main altar stands an alabaster window that serves as one of the main focal points of the entire basilica. The window depicts a dove—a biblical symbol for the Holy Spirit. The dove window captures our attention from many points throughout the basilica, symbolizing how the Holy Spirit gives life to the whole Catholic Church, most especially through her teaching ministry and the sacraments.

The light from the window first shines over a commemorative chair of Saint Peter, recalling his preaching in Rome and reminding us of how the Holy Spirit continues to guide the Church today through Peter's successors, the popes. The dove window also can be seen from the main altar where the Mass is celebrated, symbolizing how the Holy Spirit nourishes us through the sacraments. And the dove window beckons the basilica's pilgrims nearer for a closer look, reminding us of how the Holy Spirit guides and enlightens our lives.

In this way, the radiance from the dove window illuminating St. Peter's Basilica beautifully shows how the Holy Spirit animates the very life of the Catholic Church. The Spirit is, indeed, the Lord and Giver of life, building, animating, and sanctifying the Church.

Justification

One last topic worth exploring here is how the Holy Spirit communicates to us all that Jesus accomplished for us in his death and Resurrection. Christ's work of salvation is applied to our lives through his Spirit that's poured into our hearts.

But Catholic Christianity emphasizes that this work of redemption entails much more than forgiveness of sin. Jesus certainly came to save us *from* sin, but he also came to save us *for* something. He saved us so that we might share in his very life and live as sons and daughters of the Father. Christ saved us for sonship. If Jesus only came to forgive our sins, we could be reconciled with the Father. We could be restored to a right relationship with God, but we wouldn't live *in* Christ, sharing in God's trinitarian life.

Let's consider an analogy to help clarify this point. If a neighbor did something to hurt you—say, he stole your car or threw stones at your windows—he would no longer be in a right relationship with you. Your friendship would be severely broken and in need of repair. If your friend sincerely apologized for his actions, that would be a first step toward reconciliation. If he gave back the car or repaired your windows, that would be another step. If he performed many additional acts of kindness, expressed deep sorrow, and did everything he could to show his love for you to try to make amends, you probably would be friends with him again. But no matter what he did to work toward reconciliation, you probably wouldn't legally adopt him and write him into your will. You could have a right relationship with him again, but you probably wouldn't invite him into your very family life.

Yet, that is, in many ways, what God does with us. God doesn't just forgive us. He doesn't just restore us to a right relationship with him. He invites us into his very trinitarian family life. In other words, God doesn't merely pardon us like a merciful judge. He also adopts us as his children. Indeed, Saint Paul tells us that the Son was sent to free us from the slavery of sin, so that we might *become* his sons and daughters and receive the great inheritance of living with him forever in heaven. "God sent forth his Son ... to redeem those who were under the law, so that we might receive adoption as sons. And because you are sons, God has sent the Spirit of his Son into our hearts, crying 'Abba! Father!' So through God you are no longer a slave but a son, and if a son then an heir" (Gal 4:4–7).

This process of receiving the gift of salvation in Christ Jesus is called justification. The Catholic Church has described justification as the transfer from being a son of Adam to being a son of God.[2] This involves a twofold movement: dying to one's old, sinful self and being born into new life in Christ. We share in Christ's death by turning away from sin, receiving God's forgiveness, and being freed from our sinful patterns of living. But we also share in Christ's Resurrection by receiving new life in Christ. God actually conforms us to his own righteousness, making us like him, inwardly just.

And here again is the Catholic *realism* of our divine sonship. God doesn't overlook our sins and weaknesses and merely declare us to be righteous sons even though we really aren't. Rather, God truly transforms us interiorly. Through the grace of the Holy Spirit, he really changes us. He fills us with Christ's life, so that we grow in the love of Christ and become holy. And the more we cooperate with this grace, the more we grow in our life as sons and daughters of the Father, imitating the virtues of the Son of God himself.

Faith or Works?

Catholics and Protestants have long argued over the role of faith and works in the process of justification. Some Protestants are concerned that Catholics put too much emphasis

[2] The Council of Trent, Decree on Justification, January 1547, chap. 4.

St. Peter's Basilica, interior, Vatican City

on doing good works. Justification is a free gift, they say, and there is nothing we can do to earn our way to heaven. We just need to have faith. People holding this view affirm that we should strive to obey God's commandments and that good works may be a sign of God's Spirit alive in a Christian, but they are not essential for our salvation. Jesus won our salvation on the cross. We only need to welcome him as our Lord and Savior and accept his gift of salvation.

Catholics, on the other hand, are concerned that some Protestants overemphasize faith to the neglect of good works. Jesus himself taught that we need to do more than accept him as Lord. We must also obey the will of God if we want to go to heaven: "Not everyone who says ... 'Lord, Lord,' shall enter the kingdom of heaven, but he who does the will of my Father" (Mt 7:21). The New Testament letter of James similarly states, "[M]an is justified by works and not by faith alone" (Jas 2:24).

But when we consider this issue through the biblical lens of divine sonship, there may be more common ground on this issue than most realize, and the Catholic view on faith and works can begin to make more sense, even to many Protestants.

First, the Catholic Church actually emphasizes that the initial grace of justification is a completely free gift. There is nothing we can do to force God to make us his sons or daughters, just as there is nothing we did to become sons and daughters in our own natural families. We were simply born into them. Similarly, there is nothing we can do to merit our status as God's children. The initiative belongs to God, who freely forgives us and fills us with his life. This is what the *Catechism of the Catholic Church* stresses: "*No one can merit the initial grace* of forgiveness and justification, at the beginning of conversion" (*CCC* 2010; emphasis in original).

But at the same time, while the initial grace of divine sonship is a completely free gift, we must grow and mature as God's sons and daughters. We must be conformed to Christ, living ever more like the Son himself. And that involves allowing Christ's love to radiate through us, or what we commonly call "good works". But even our good works are not entirely our own. They are inspired by the promptings of the Spirit. They involve cooperating with God's grace. God takes the initiative and engages our free will, inviting us to say yes in the many opportunities he gives us to grow in his love.

Moreover, the Catholic Church teaches that this gift of salvation is one that must be cared for, cultivated, and deepened. As in any relationship, our friendship with God could become stagnant and lukewarm over time if we're not seeking to grow in the love of Christ. Moreover, if we're not careful, we could even do something that would break our relationship with the Father. The Bible is full of images that make this point: We could become a prodigal son who becomes "lost" and "dead" to the Father. We could become the kind of person Jesus describes in the parable of the sower who receives God's Word with joy, but when trials and persecution arises, he immediately falls away. We could be the disciples who call Jesus "Lord", but do not serve him in the poor and suffering and are not allowed into heaven (see Mt 25:31–46). No matter what sins we commit, there is always the possibility of turning back to God, receiving his loving mercy, and being restored in his life. But the point in these cases is that if someone actually has turned away from Christ's salvation, one is in need of his mercy, and one has lost the life of God in him. We should never presume upon our salvation.

Take Heed Lest You Fall

One analogy from the writings of Saint Paul that expresses this point best is how the Christian life is like the Israelites' journey to the Promised Land in the Exodus—a journey in which people might receive the gift of salvation but lose it if they are not faithful.

In his First Letter to the Corinthians, Paul emphasizes how God saved "all" the Israelites from slavery in Egypt, but "most of them" did not enter the Promised Land (see 1 Cor 10:1–5). He tells how God miraculously parted the waters of the Red Sea so the people could escape from Egypt and how God provided food and drink for them in their journey through the desert. But Paul goes on to stress that God was not pleased with most of them. In fact, many fell into sin and idolatry in the desert and were disinherited. Note how they *all* received the same free gift of being saved from slavery, but *most of them* lost that gift and were not allowed to enter the Promised Land.

Paul then goes on to say that "these things happened to them as a warning" for us. In other words, they were recorded in Scripture "for our instruction" (1 Cor 10:11). Paul is telling the Corinthian Christians, and all of us, that what happened to the Israelites in the desert could happen to us in our own journey of faith. We must not presume upon the gift of our salvation. Just because we have received Christ's saving grace doesn't mean we automatically will go to heaven. We must be faithful to that gift. Just as many of those Israelites turned away from God and were not allowed to enter the Promised Land, so we Christians will be disinherited from the Promised Land of heaven if we do not remain faithful. Paul warns, "[L]et any one who thinks that he stands take heed lest he fall" (1 Cor 10:12).

So in summary, there is a distinction between what one might call "getting in" and "staying in". "Getting in" to God's covenant family is a completely free gift. The initial grace of justification—forgiveness of sins and becoming God's sons and daughters—is freely bestowed on us by the Father. There is nothing we can do to earn it. But "staying in" covenant with God comes with great responsibility. We must be faithful to the covenant family life. We must never presume on our salvation, thinking we could never turn away from this gift. Cooperating with God's grace, we must endeavor to grow and mature as God's children, living ever more in imitation of Christ.

Chapter Seven

Why Do I Need the Church?

Imagine if you were one of the twelve apostles there that day when Jesus said to Peter, "[Y]ou are Peter, and on this rock I will build my Church.... I will give you the keys of the kingdom of heaven" (Mt 16:18–19). What would these words have meant to you?

For a first-century Jew, the image of the keys of the kingdom would have been charged with great symbolism. In the ancient biblical tradition, the king had a right-hand man, a prime minister or master of the palace, who was in charge of the day-to-day affairs of the kingdom. In the book of Isaiah, chapter 22, the king's steward is described as wearing a royal robe, holding an office with authority, and serving as "a father to the inhabitants of Jerusalem" (Is 22:21). And the chief symbol for the prime minister's authority was the keys of the kingdom (see Is 22:22).

So when Jesus goes from village to village announcing a kingdom, and then one day says to Peter, "I give you the keys of the kingdom," he is saying a lot. He's establishing Peter as his principle leader in his kingdom, like the prime minster, the one who would be in charge of the affairs of the kingdom. And this prime-minister-like role was passed on to Peter's successors, the popes, throughout the centuries to serve as a source of unity in the Church and a guardian of all that Christ had revealed.

But some people today might wonder whether they really need an authoritative teacher and guide to show them the way to God. "I'm really more spiritual than religious," some might say. "Why do I need a Church? Can't I just make up my own path to God?" For them, the Church is just an organization—at best, a kind of spiritual club that offers support for those who want that sort of thing, but certainly not for everyone. "I'm a good person," some may argue. "I believe in God. I'm nice to people. Does God really care whether I'm a part of the Church?"

The Mystery of the Church

When we hear the word "church" today, many of us might have images of a building with a cross, an altar, and a priest. Or we might envision a massive worldwide organization, or the Vatican in Rome—or even the pope.

But when Jesus, in response to Peter's confession of faith, announced the establishment of his Church, he used a term that has great significance in the Bible. He spoke of his *ekklesia*: "[O]n this rock I will build my Church [*ekklesia*]." The word means "gathering" or "assembly", and it's derived from *ek kalein*, which means "to call out of".

In the ancient Greek Old Testament, Israel was called God's *ekklesia*. The idea is that God *called out* Israel from all the nations, called them out of slavery in Egypt, and gathered them together at Mount Sinai to become the chosen people, a special "possession among all peoples" (Ex 19:5). They

St. Peter's Basilica, interior, Vatican City

were gathered into a new relationship with God, a special belonging to the Lord (see *CCC* 751).

Jesus, therefore, makes a profound statement when he talks about establishing his Church (*ekklesia*). His community of followers is not about individuals organizing a movement, rallying together for a common cause, or calling meetings for friendship and support. Jesus makes clear that *he* is the one taking the initiative. "[Y]ou did not choose me, but I chose you" (Jn 15:16). His messianic community is the result of a divine "calling together". Just as God called Israel out of slavery in Egypt and gathered them together as his chosen people, so Jesus calls us out (*ek kalein*) of a much deeper slavery: a slavery to sin. He liberates us from our pride, vanity, greed, selfishness, and control, so that we might be gathered together in a new way of life in him as the new people of God, the Church (*ekklesia*).

Communion with Christ

The purpose of Christ's calling all people together is to share in the unity he has with the Father and the Holy Spirit. As we saw in chapter 7, Jesus wants to send his Spirit into our hearts so that we might have his divine life in us—so that we might participate, by grace, in the unity of the Father, Son, and Holy Spirit. All who share in this divine communion also share in a most profound fellowship with each other—one that goes beyond mere human friendship. It is rooted in their fellowship with God: "[T]hat which we have seen and heard we proclaim also to you, so that you may have fellowship with us; and our fellowship is with the Father and with his Son Jesus Christ" (1 Jn 1:3).

This communion in Christ that unites believers together lies at the very heart of the Catholic Church. Underneath the various human, visible structures of the Church—the pope, bishops, and priests in the hierarchy, and the various teachings, programs, rituals, and schedules—lies the invisible mystical fellowship of all who are in full communion with Jesus Christ and thus in full communion with each other.

This is why the New Testament calls the Church the "body of Christ" (1 Cor 12:12) with the various members of the body each sharing in the life of its head, Jesus. The Church is also called the Bride of Christ in the sense that Christ and the Church form one unity, one body, just as husband and wife become one in marriage. So intimate is this unity that the Church is even identified with Christ himself. When Jesus appeared to Saul of Tarsus, who was persecuting the Christians, he said to him, "Saul, Saul, why do you per-secute me?" (Acts 9:4). Notice how Jesus didn't ask why Saul was persecuting "the Church" or "the Christians". Jesus so intimately identifies himself with his community of disciples, that what Saul does to the Church he does to Christ. That's why Jesus asks him, "[W]hy do you persecute *me*?"

The Vine and the Branches

A twelfth-century mosaic in the Basilica of San Clemente in Rome beautifully illustrates this point in what can be seen as an artistic meditation on Jesus' words at the Last Supper: "I am the vine, you are the branches" (Jn 15:5).

At the mosaic's center is the crucified Christ. But the cross on which he hangs is actually a tree, indeed, a tree of life. Growing out from the roots and limbs of this tree is a network of branches that swirl around, reaching out to the whole world, drawing people of all walks of life into itself. We see priests, theologians, and saints, as well as peasants, a farm girl feeding her animals, and a shepherd petting his dog. All are united to Christ and, thus, to each other. The world is God's vineyard. Christ is the vine. And we are the branches. All are caught up into this full communion with Christ, which is the Church.

I like to imagine Jesus in the mosaic reaching out to us today through one of the branches swirling down toward us, inviting us to share in the rich life of the vine, the Church. Will we join ourselves to Christ? Will we allow ourselves to enter deeply into the communion of life Jesus offers? The question of whether one joins the Church is not about deciding which religious club, if any, I like the most. Rather, it is about Jesus calling us: calling us out of

ourselves (*ek kalein*) and inviting us to a new way of life, to
see as he sees, to love as he loves. We can only do that by
sharing in the fullness of his life and love, or as Vatican II
put it, that "fullness grace and truth"[1] that Christ entrusted
to the Catholic Church.

The Church Is One

Traditionally, there are four characteristics or "marks" of the
Church that Christ founded. The Church is one, holy, Catholic, and apostolic. Christ makes these four essential features
of the Church present, and their manifestation throughout
history serve as a sign pointing to the unique work Christ
does in the world through the Church.

The first mark of the Church is that it is one. This points
to the deep unity Jesus intended his followers to have. So
important was this for Jesus, that the night before he died, he
prayed to his heavenly Father for all Christians "that they may
all be one; even as you, Father, are in me, and I in you, that
they also may be in us, so that the world may believe that you
have sent me" (Jn 17:21). Think about these words. Jesus has
in mind much more than a vague unity of people who get
along, share some common ideas, and work on a few projects
together. He prays that Christians may be one *even as he and
the Father are one.* We saw how profound the unity is between
the Father and the Son. *That's* the kind of unity he calls us to
participate in! Indeed, Christ's model for Christian unity is
nothing less than the supreme unity of the Holy Trinity.

This is why Saint Paul can be so adamant about the one-
ness of the Church. Paul emphasizes that "God is one" and

---

[1] Vatican II, Decree on Ecumenism, *Unitatis Redintegratio*, November 21,
1964, no. 3.

"you are all one in Christ Jesus" (Gal 3:20, 28). He exhorts Christ's followers to be of "one mind striving side by side for the faith" (Phil 1:27). The Church herself is "one body" (Eph 2:16): "There is one body and one Spirit ... one hope ... one Lord, one faith, one baptism, one God and Father of us all" (Eph 4:4–6).

But this idea of the Church's unity isn't the genius of Saint Paul or even something Jesus invented at the Last Supper. It's the fulfillment of the Father's plan from the beginning of time. From the start of creation, God intended all humanity to be united with him in one covenant family. We've seen how sin didn't just separate us from God, but it also divided us against each other. Jesus came to reunite the divided human family, to restore that twofold unity that God originally intended us to have with him *and with each other*. The fullness of that unity is found in the Church.

Visible Unity

Let's go back in time to the early Church, and we will see how from the very first centuries of Christianity, the Church's unity was exhibited visibly in three main ways: common belief, common worship, and apostolic succession (see *CCC* 815).

First, there was a *common belief* among all the faithful. The early Christians professed that one faith was received from the apostles. As the second-century bishop Ireneaus of Lyons said,

> For the Churches which have been planted in Germany do not believe or hand down anything different, nor do those in Spain, nor those in Gaul, nor those in the East, nor those in Egypt, nor those in Libya, nor those which have been established in the central regions of the world. But as the

Basilica of San Clemente, interior, Rome

sun, that creature of God, is one and the same throughout
the whole world, so also the preaching of the truth shines
everywhere, and enlightens all men that are willing to come
to a knowledge of the truth.[2]

This common set of central beliefs came to be summed up in
the early Church's creeds—summary statements of the essential elements of the faith. These served as a source of unity
for all Christians and were intended especially for people preparing for baptism. How did early converts to Christianity
know if the faith they professed was in harmony with what
Jesus and the apostles proclaimed? They turned to the Creed,
which ensured communion with that apostolic faith.

[2] St. Ireneaus, *Adv. Haeres* I, 10, 2.

The second visible bond of unity was a *common celebration of worship*. While there were diverse expressions in the Church's liturgical practices, Christians throughout the world all had certain essential common elements in their worship of God, most especially baptism and the Eucharist. There weren't large groups of Christians saying baptism is necessary, with others viewing it as just an option, and still others opposing baptism. All Christians throughout the world celebrated baptism as the gateway into the Christian life. Similarly, there wasn't diversity of opinion on whether the Lord's Supper should be celebrated. Christians throughout the world were united in the common worship of God in the Eucharist.

The third visible bond of unity was *apostolic succession*. The early Christians were united around the leadership of their local bishop, who was seen, not just as an appointed leader, but someone who was given authority by Christ. As we will see, Jesus gave authority to his apostles to lead the Church, and that authority was passed on to their successors throughout the centuries. Through ordination, the bishop today stands in the long line of "apostolic succession" going back to the first apostles themselves. Vested with this authority, the bishops lead the people in their local vicinity in teaching, worship, and maintaining fraternal concord. Each bishop himself is united with all other bishops through his union with the bishop of Rome, the pope.

Wounds to Unity

While there had been various tensions and divisions within Christ's Church along the way, the unity of all Christians was exhibited in the world beautifully for over one thousand years. God's people were united in a common faith and a common worship, as well as through their local bishops in apostolic succession. In later centuries, however, "much more serious dissensions appeared and large communities became separated from full communion with the Catholic Church" (*CCC* 817).

One of the most significant breaks from this unity came in the 1500s with Martin Luther and what has been called the Protestant Reformation. This represented a rupture on all three levels of belief, worship, and apostolic succession. While there were many factors involved, one of the chief tenants of Protestantism at the root of this separation was the belief in *sola scriptura*—the idea that the Bible alone is the only infallible authority for Christian faith. In this new view, an individual should go to the Bible alone to learn what God has revealed. One does not need the teaching authority of the Church or Sacred Tradition. The Holy Spirit will guide each individual to understand God's truth in Scripture.

But it was clear from the very beginning that this new approach would not work. Some Protestant leaders interpreted the Bible one way, while others interpreted it in different directions on matters they considered so serious that they broke away from each other and started new churches. And then those communities further fractured when they came to disagree with each other on what they believed were essential matters of faith. This splintering has happened thousands of times since the rise of Protestantism, so that today, according to the *World Christian Encyclopedia*, there are over thirty-three thousand different Christian denominations—thousands of groups disagreeing with each other on some point that, at least in their eyes, warranted the start of a new church.

This is a far cry from the unity that Jesus prayed for when he prayed that Christians would be one even as he and the Father are one. Such division stands in stark contrast today with the one Catholic Church throughout the world that continues to be united in one faith, a common worship, and apostolic succession.

Highlighting the sad disunity that has emerged in the last five hundred years is not to point fingers. It's important to note that when it comes to these divisions, as the *Catechism* affirms, "often enough, men of both sides were to blame".[3] And people today who are born into these communities cannot be held responsible for the separation that the original leaders of their communities sowed centuries ago (see *CCC* 818). We must do all we can to foster unity. After all, there is much that unites Catholic and Protestant Christians: the love of God, belief in Jesus, the Bible, prayer, and certain moral convictions, to name a few. Baptized Protestant Christians are truly incorporated into Christ; they are brothers and sisters in Christ. And there are many ways in which their lives can inspire us to love Christ more, love Scripture more, and share the gospel more. Indeed, Christ's Spirit is at work in them, and there are "elements of sanctification and of truth"[4] in their communities. Those positive elements should be a source of unity and stepping stones toward "the fullness of grace and truth" that Jesus has entrusted to the Catholic Church (*CCC* 819).

Holy

The second mark of the Church is that it is holy. But what does this mean? How can the Church be holy if many of her members, even leaders, are sinful?

[3] *CCC* 817, quoting Vatican II, Decree on Ecumenism, *Unitatis Redintegratio*, November 21, 1964, no. 3.

[4] *CCC* 819, quoting Vatican II, Dogmatic Constitution on the Church, *Lumen Gentium*, November 21, 1964, no. 8.

From the *Symbolon* series

The "Arms" of St. Peter's Square, Vatican City

The Church is called holy not because all of her members are holy but because God's power remains at work in the Church despite the sinfulness of her people. It is the Lord's holiness that becomes present among sinful men through the Church. The Church is the bearer of Christ's holiness to the world. As Vatican II explained, the Church has "the fullness of the means of salvation".[5]

Still, some may wonder how the Church could possibly be an instrument of holiness if there have been some lay leaders, priests, bishops, and even popes who have lived far from impeccable lives. This is a fair question, and one that has been raised before. There have been some in the history of Christianity who believed that only sinless people can be instruments

---

[5] *CCC* 824, quoting *Unitatis Redintegratio*, no. 3.

of God's grace. But since the time of Saint Augustine the Catholic tradition has explained that Christ can communicate his grace even through unworthy instruments. The passing on of Christ's holiness is not dependent on the holiness of the minister (see *CCC* 1128). Christ's holiness is present through the "fullness of the means of salvation", which he entrusted to the Church: the Scriptures, the sacraments, the teachings, and the witness and prayers of the saints. Christ endowed the Catholic Church with the fullness of grace and truth to make us holy. And it is Jesus who, through the visible, human elements of the Church, transforms us sinners into mature sons and daughters of God.

Catholic

The word "Catholic" means "universal" or "in keeping with the whole". The Church is called Catholic in two senses.

First, Jesus entrusted the Church with "the fullness of the means of salvation". The Church is Catholic, in "keeping with the whole", in the sense that it has the fullness of what Jesus wants us to have to know him and love him: the complete confession of faith, the full life of all the sacraments, and the ordained ministers who continue Christ's work through apostolic succession.

The Church is also called Catholic in terms of her mission to the whole human race. Remember that Jesus' work of salvation entailed gathering people back, not just in relationship with the Father, but also in relationship with each other. That full communion is found in the Church. The Catholic Church, therefore, reaches out to the entire world, gathering peoples of all nations, races, and languages back into the one covenant family of God (see *CCC* 831).

Apostolic

The Church is called "apostolic" because she is founded on the apostles and continues to be guided by the apostles through their successors. This is the idea of apostolic succession.

There was an ancient Jewish rabbinic saying: "A man's envoy is like the man himself." At a key turning point in Jesus' public ministry, he chose twelve apostles and made them his envoys. He gave them authority to do what he had been doing: teaching and healing (see Mt 10:1–8). And he later commissioned them to make disciples of all nations, giving them the authority to teach and baptize in his name (see Mt 28:18–20). The word "apostle", in fact, means "one who is sent", and the New Testament depicts the apostles as Christ's envoys, emissaries who represent the sender. So closely associated with Jesus were the apostles that he told them, "He who hears you hears me, and he who rejects you rejects me, and he who rejects me rejects him who sent me" (Lk 10:16).

That's why they are called in the New Testament "ambassadors for Christ" (2 Cor 5:20) and "heralds" or authorized spokesmen (*keryx*). Paul made this point in his First Letter to the Thessalonians. The apostles' word was considered to be conveying God's word: "[W]hen you received the word of God which you heard from us, you accepted it not as the words of men but as what it really is, the word of God" (1 Thess 2:13).

This authority which Christ gave the apostles, however, was not only for the original twelve men. It was passed on to their successors. The New Testament shows how the apostles left behind others to continue their work. Shortly after Christ's Ascension, Peter and the apostles chose a man named Matthias to be the successor for Judas, taking Judas' place "in this ministry and apostleship" (Acts 1:25). Saint

Paul appointed elders in every church in Asia Minor—people who continued his apostolic work after he completed his mission there (see Acts 14:23). And Paul told his own disciples to do the same. He instructed Titus to appoint leaders in every town, an indication that the authority of Paul was passing from his disciple Titus down to a third generation of leaders in the Church (see Tit 1:5). And these elders were not merely assistants or figurehead positions. They had real authority to rule and make decisions and were even known to heal the sick and forgive sins (see Acts 15:22–23; 16:4; 1 Tim 5:17; Jas 5:14).

We can see the idea of apostolic succession even after New Testament times in the first generations of Christians *after* the apostles. The first-century bishop Clement of Rome (c. A.D. 96), for example, explained how the apostles "appointed their first converts, after testing them by the Spirit, to be bishops and deacons for the believers of the future".[6] He says it shouldn't be surprising that the apostles to whom God entrusted such an important mission for the whole world would have appointed successors and then instructed their successors to do the same: "They proceeded to appoint the ministers I spoke of, and they went on to add an instruction that if these should fall asleep, other accredited persons should succeed them in their office."[7]

Similarly, Ignatius of Antioch (c. 107) noted the authority of the bishop. He wrote about how the office of bishop is conferred by God[8] and stressed the importance of "obedience to your bishop" and never breaking away from your bishop.[9] "Where the bishop is to be seen, there let all his people be;

[6] Clement of Rome, Letter to the Corinthians, 42.
[7] Ibid., 44.
[8] Ignatius of Antioch, Letter to Philadelphia, 1.
[9] Ignatius of Antioch, Letter to the Smyrneans, 2.

Guiding Star Pilgrimages

The Apostles Peter & Paul, Basilica of St. Paul
Outside the Walls, Rome

just as wherever Jesus Christ is present, we have the Catholic Church."[10]

This apostolic authority was passed on from one generation to the next throughout the centuries through the ordination of bishops. The bishops today stand in this two-thousand-year unbroken line of apostolic succession. They serve as central points of unity for Christ's followers in their role of teaching, governing, and leading the people in worship.

So let's remember what Jesus said to the apostles: "He who hears you hears me, and he who rejects you rejects me" (Lk 10:16). This is no small matter. Jesus views himself as having such a close connection with his apostles that he associates acceptance of his apostles with acceptance of him! Imagine what would happen if someone in Galilee told Jesus, "I love

[10] Ibid., 8.

you, but I can't stand Peter and the other apostles.... I want a relationship with you, Jesus, but I don't want your Church." To the extent people rejected the apostles, they were rejecting Christ.

Something similar could be said of the successors of the apostles, the bishops, today. To the extent that we welcome the apostles' successors, we are welcoming Christ himself. This is also why Vatican II explained, "The bishops have by divine institution taken the place of the apostles as pastors of the Church,... and whoever despises them despises Christ and him who sent Christ".[11]

Infallibility

The *Catechism* affirms that Jesus gave a share of his own infallibility to the pope and the body of bishops united with him. He did this to ensure that the faith was handed on purely with the assistance of the Holy Spirit from one generation to the next. Jesus had said he would build his Church upon Peter, and the gates of hell would not prevail against it (see Mt 16:18). And he prayed that Peter's faith would not fail him and that he would be a source of strength for his brethren (see Lk 22:32). Catholics believe that the gift of Peter's unifying faith was passed on from Peter to his successors, the popes, who would serve as a source of strength for Christ's followers throughout the centuries.

But the Catholic view of infallibility does not mean that the pope never makes any errors when teaching, or that he can predict next year's Super Bowl winner, or that he is flawless in his administrative skills, or that he is sinless in

---

[11] *CCC* 862, quoting *Lumen Gentium*, no. 20.

his living. The gift of infallibility relates only to when the pope teaches definitively, in his office as the supreme pastor of all the faithful, a doctrine related to faith and morals (see *CCC* 888–92).

This is an incredible gift for the Church as a whole—and one that makes a lot of sense. We've seen how the Bible on its own is open to an array of interpretations. It cannot all by itself resolve disputes about how it should be explained. It's fitting that God would provide the Church with a living voice to settle disputes about Scripture and to ensure correct interpretation of all that Jesus revealed. That living voice is found in Peter's successors, the popes.

The Church of Me?

Some people today, however, do not want an authoritative teacher, a pope, or a Church at all. They say that they are spiritual, but not religious—that they believe in God, but don't need the Church.

One danger, however, of seeking God all on our own, apart from the Church, is that we make God in our own image and likeness; it's too easy to tailor a spirituality and morality that suits our own comforts, lifestyles, and interests. After all, being "spiritual but not religious" would be a very appealing option for someone who still wants to have some sense of God in his life—someone whose conscience is uneasy about rejecting God entirely—but who wants to keep God at arm's reach and still do his own thing.

In such a case, it's easier to create my own religious and moral values—values that are comfortable for me—than it is to accept the revelation of Jesus Christ and the teachings of a Church that calls me to ongoing conversion. Rather than follow a moral standard outside myself—one that calls me on to greater responsibility, commitment to others, generosity, and sacrificial love—I can determine for myself what is right and wrong. I can craft my own beliefs and values that conveniently justify my current way of living. In the world of being "spiritual but not religious", I can make myself my own pope in my own religion: the Church of Me.

But Jesus invites us to something greater. He calls us out of ourselves. Remember this is what the word "church" (*ekklesia*) at its root means: to call out of (*ek kalein*). Jesus calls us out of our limited perspectives and selfish pursuits, so that we can go beyond ourselves and experience the joy that comes from living for God and for others, the joy that comes from living like him in total self-giving love.

We can't separate Jesus from his Church. In other words, we can't say that we love the king but don't accept his kingdom, or that we love Christ but reject his Church. When we willfully separate ourselves from Christ's Church, we separate ourselves from Christ himself. When we pick and choose which teachings of the Church *we* want to follow, we're in the end picking and choosing what we want to do instead of fully allowing Christ's teachings to shape our lives.

Jesus invites us today to surrender whatever willfulness might be keeping us from fully entrusting our lives to his loving plan—his plan that has been faithfully passed on for two thousand years through the Catholic Church. Jesus invites us to be drawn more closely to him through the Church. Will you join yourself to Jesus by living more intimately in the vine and the branches of Christ and the Church?

Chapter Eight

Mary and the Saints

The Basilica of St. Mary Major's in Rome is the principle church dedicated to Mary in the entire world. Practically everything in this basilica points to something about Mary and her important role in the Christian life.

Paintings, mosaics, and statues take us on a tour of Mary's life. We move from the angel Gabriel's announcement to her that she would be the Mother of the Messiah to her standing at Calvary watching her Son die on the cross. Behind the main altar, an image invites us to contemplate Mary's own last moments on earth, while the majestic mosaic above celebrates Mary being crowned by her Son as queen of heaven and earth.

Catholics throughout the world come to this beautiful church to honor Mary, the Mother of God, and ask for her prayers. But all this focus on Mary invites us to take a closer look at Catholic Marian devotion: Why do Catholics give so much attention to Mary? And why would they dedicate a whole basilica to her? Does devotion to Mary distract us from a personal relationship with Christ? These are some of the questions we will explore as we consider what Catholics really believe about Mary—and why.

Facade, Basilica of St. Mary Major, Rome

"Behold, Your Mother!"

Just before Jesus died on Calvary, he gave us one last gift. With his beloved disciple, John, and his Mother, Mary, standing at the foot the cross, Jesus said to Mary, "Woman, behold, your son!" and then said to the disciple, "Behold, your mother!" (Jn 19:26–27). In doing so, the dying Jesus put the two in a new relationship, entrusting his Mother into his disciple's care.

But when read in light of the whole of Scripture, these sacred words of Jesus point to something more. For the beloved disciple, John, plays a unique role in the Bible. In John's Gospel, where individual characters often embody larger groups, the beloved disciple stands as a representative for all faithful disciples. He's the one who leans closest to Jesus at the Last Supper (see Jn 13:25). He's the only apostle who remains with Jesus at the cross on Good Friday, while all the others fled (see Jn 19:26). The beloved disciple is the first to believe in the Resurrection of Jesus (see Jn 20:8), and he's the one who bears witness to the risen Christ (see Jn 21:7, 24). The beloved disciple is traditionally understood to be the individual apostle Saint John, but in the fourth Gospel, he also represents all faithful disciples of the Lord.

This sheds important light on Jesus' mysterious words to the beloved disciple from the cross: "Behold, your mother!" With these words, Jesus puts Mary and the beloved disciple into a new Mother-Son relationship. But there's also a deeper spiritual meaning. Since the beloved disciple represents all faithful disciples, this passage has often been interpreted as pointing to Mary as the spiritual Mother for all Christians (*CCC* 968–70). In other words, Mary, as the Mother of the beloved disciple, should be seen as the Mother of all the faithful followers of Christ, whom the beloved disciple represents.

This is one reason why Catholics refer to Mary as our spiritual Mother. We Christian disciples truly have the life of Christ in us. Jesus' Mother, therefore, becomes our spiritual Mother by grace. And what a blessing it is to have such a spiritual Mother! She who said yes to God's will and welcomed the Son of God into her womb—she who is so close to her Son, Jesus—prays for us, that we may say yes to God and welcome Christ ever more into our own daily lives.

Treat Her Like a Queen?

Ever since the early Church, Christians also have honored Mary as queen. In sacred art she often appears with a crown on her head. Prayers and hymns venerate her as enthroned in heaven, reigning with her Son. Indeed, the Catholic Church teaches that Mary is the queen in Christ's kingdom.

But why do Catholics treat Mary like a queen? This early Christian practice is actually rooted in Scripture—in the biblical tradition of the queen mother. In ancient Israel and other ancient Near Eastern kingdoms, it was not the king's *wife* who reigned as queen, but the king's *mother*. Most kings back then, unfortunately, had many wives. King Solomon, for example, had seven hundred wives and three hundred concubines. The queenship couldn't be given to one thousand women. But each king only had one mother, and the queenship was bestowed on her.

The office of the queen mother was not just some honorific, figurehead position. She had real royal authority. As a member of the royal court, the queen mother sat on a throne, wore a crown, and shared in the king's authority to lead (see 2 Kings 24:12; Jer 13:18–20). Most of all, she also served as an advocate for the people. Citizens of the kingdom would bring their petitions to the queen mother, knowing that she would present them to her royal son.

We can see the queen mother's intercessory role in the way the Bible contrasts the wife of the king and the king's mother. In 1 Kings 1, for example, we read about a woman named Bathsheba who is the wife of King David. When she wants to visit her royal husband's chamber, she has to bow down before him and pay him homage (see 1 Kings 1:16–17, 31).

But in the next chapter of the Bible, Bathsheba is treated very differently. King David has died, and now Bathsheba's son, Solomon, is reigning as king. That makes Bathsheba the queen mother. As queen mother, when she enters the royal chamber to visit her kingly son, she doesn't have to stand

From the Symbolon series

Basilica of St. Mary Major, interior, Rome

up and bow down before him. The opposite occurs. King Solomon stands up and bows down before *her*, honoring her as queen mother. He even orders a throne to be brought in for her to sit upon, and that throne is placed at his right hand, which in the Bible is the position of authority (see 1 Kings 2:19). Most interestingly, we see Bathsheba bringing the king a petition from one of the citizens of the kingdom. Solomon says to her, "Make your request, my mother; for I will not refuse you" (1 Kings 2:20)—demonstrating how the queen mother's intercessory role normally worked.[1]

This scriptural queen mother background sheds light on why Catholics honor Mary as queen and why they bring petitions to her. As the Mother of the King, Jesus Christ,

---

[1] On the unique circumstances surrounding this petition and how it was received, see Edward Sri, *Queen Mother: A Biblical Theology of Mary's Queenship* (Steubenville, Ohio: Emmaus Road Publishing, 2004), 52–53.

Mary would be seen from a biblical perspective as the queen mother. And as queen mother, she serves as an advocate for the people. That's one reason why Catholics seek her intercession, trusting that she, like the queen mothers of old, will present our needs to her royal Son, Jesus.

But even with this rich biblical background, many good Christians still might feel uncomfortable about honoring Mary and seeking her intercession. Some might worry that to do so would distract us from a relationship with Christ. Others might even worry that Catholic devotion to Mary is a form of idolatry, worshipping Mary instead of God alone. Here, we must address two common fundamental questions people have about Mary: Do Catholics worship Mary? And, why do Catholics pray to Mary? The answers to these questions will shed light on Catholic devotion to the saints as a whole.

Do Catholics Worship Mary?

Here we must be clear. Catholics don't worship Mary, but we do honor her. Worship is the homage and praise given to God alone for who he is as the divine being. But honor is something different. Honor is the respect we give when recognizing a certain excellence in a person. Christians honor people all the time for good grades, athletic victories, and other achievements, successes, and qualities. From a Christian perspective, when we honor people, we ultimately are recognizing the great things God has accomplished in a person's life.

So when Catholics honor Mary and the other saints, we are simply recognizing the great things God has done in their lives and celebrating it. This in no way takes away from the attention we give to God. In fact, it gives God more praise. After all, who praises the artist more, the person who focuses only on the artist himself while ignoring his works of art? Or the person who praises the artist by admiring his masterpieces? God is the divine artist, and we should praise him for his greatest masterpieces, the saints. The fact that God can take individual persons and transform them with his grace and make them saints is, indeed, praiseworthy! So if the Bible often praises God for his natural works of creation—praising God for the sun, moon, mountains, and seas (see Ps 104)—how much more should we praise God for his supernatural works of creation: Mary, and the saints? Honoring the saints does not detract in any way from our worship of God. We actually give God *more praise* when we acknowledge his achievements in the saints. This is especially true when it comes to Mary. As the Mother of Jesus and our queen mother, Mary has the highest place of honor among all the saints.

Why Do Catholics Pray to Mary?

Catholics don't pray to Mary like we pray to the Holy Trinity. Mary is not God. But we do ask Mary and the saints for prayer. This is the idea of intercession. Just as we might ask a friend for prayer in a time of need, so we can ask for prayers from our brothers and sisters who have gone before us, the saints. The only difference is that Mary and the saints are in heaven close to God's throne, so their prayers are even *more* powerful.

Mary and the saints have a profound intimacy with Jesus in heaven. Even though they have died, they are fully alive in Jesus Christ. So they remain in communion with everyone else who is united to Christ, including us Christians on earth. That's why they can hear our petitions and pray for us. It's not on their own power but through our shared communion in Christ that the saints lovingly intercede for our needs. In fact, the Bible describes people from previous eras who have long been dead—people such as Moses, Samuel, Jeremiah, and Onaias the high priest—as still having the ability to pray for God's people on earth (see 2 Mac 15:11–16; Jer 15:1). The Bible describes the saints, not as disconnected from our lives or cut off from the body of Christ, but as "a cloud of witnesses" (Heb 12:1), and their prayers in heaven play a role in God's actions on earth (cf. Rev 5:8; 8:3). Think about how much the saints love us. They have gone through the same struggles we face, and they have persevered in faith. They have fought the good fight and won the race and now share in the victorious crown of salvation. It's as if they are "in the stands" up in heaven cheering for us—praying that we persevere as they did, so that we can be with them, sharing in the blessed life of heaven.

Still, some may wonder why Catholics don't go to God directly. Why bother asking Mary and the saints for prayer if one can go straight to God with all of his needs? Here, we need to see how intercession helps us grow in love for Jesus and each other. Saint Paul commands his followers to intercede for him (see 2 Cor 1:11) and for each other (see 1 Tim 2:1). One key way we grow in love of Christ is through our love of neighbor. Just as fellowship among Christians on earth brings us closer to Christ, so also fellowship with the saints in heaven strengthens our union with Jesus (see *CCC* 957). Sharing needs and asking for prayer among Christian brethren is a powerful way to build up love in the body of Christ.

God does not get upset or feel jealous when we turn to each other in our need. What father gets angry when he sees his children grow in love and honor for each other, when he sees them turn to each other in need, help each other, and pray for each other? Such unity builds up love in the family. Similarly, God the Father rejoices when he sees his children sharing needs with each other, praying for each other, and growing in love for each other. The more fundamental question, therefore, is not whether it is okay to ask Mary and the saints to pray for us, but whether we want to love Christ with all of our hearts. If we want to give God more praise and adoration in our lives, we will love Jesus by growing in love for all of the saints, seeking their intercession as our spiritual brothers and sisters in heaven. Mary, in particular, prays for us with her maternal heart and as our queen mother serves as a loving intercessor before her Son's throne.

Immaculate Conception

Now we're ready to consider four core Catholic beliefs about Mary known as the four Marian dogmas: Mary's Immaculate Conception, her being the Mother of God, her perpetual virginity, and her Assumption to heaven. It would be a mistake, however, to think of these dogmas as being only about Mary. Though certainly related to Mary, these four Marian dogmas are actually centered on Jesus Christ. What the Church proclaims about Mary in these dogmas is intimately connected to the reality of who Jesus is. They ultimately are meant to help us know and understand Jesus and his plan of salvation better, so that we can love him all the more.

We can see this especially in the first Marian dogma to consider: the Immaculate Conception. The Catholic Church teaches that Mary was immaculately conceived, meaning that she was conceived in her mother's womb full of grace, without the stain of original sin.

St. Peter's Square, Vatican City

From the *Symbolon* series

This Marian doctrine is not as much about exalting our Lady as it is about pointing to Jesus. Mary was not given this unique privilege of being full of grace for her own sake, but for the sake of the child whom she would carry in her womb. Since Jesus is truly the all-holy Son of God, the second Person of the Trinity, Catholics believe he is worthy to dwell in a pure vessel, a holy temple. God could have entered our humanity any way he liked, but it is most fitting that he would dwell in an immaculate mother, a spotless tabernacle. If the ancient Jews used the purest of gold to build the Ark of the Covenant—the sacred vessel that carried the holy presence of God—it makes sense that God would use the purest of mothers to carry his divine Son. To prepare Mary for becoming the Mother of the Savior, God endowed her with this unique fullness of grace so that she might be a pure vessel for the Son of God (see *CCC* 490).

Much of the Church's reflection on this unique privilege of Mary flows from the extraordinary words with which the angel Gabriel greeted her at the Annunciation. He said to her, "Hail, full of grace" (Lk 1:28). No one else in the Bible had ever been honored by an angel with such a title. And the fact that the angel doesn't address Mary with her personal name, but with the title "full of grace", indicates that this expression is meant to tell us something important about our Lady.

The Greek word commonly translated "full of grace" is *kecharitomene*. The term means "graced" and describes someone who has been and continues to be graced. The expression here indicates that Mary *already* was filled with God's saving grace and that grace continues to be at work in her. This verb is also used in Ephesians 1:5–8, where it is associated with the saving, transforming power of grace that brings redemption and forgiveness of sins and makes us children of God. Here, in Luke 1:28, the verb is in the perfect tense, indicating that this saving grace was already operative in Mary's life before the angel's greeting. Though the expression does not prove that Mary was conceived full of grace, it shows that, even before Gabriel appeared to her, Mary had already been filled with God's redemptive grace.

As the early Christians pondered Mary's role in God's plan of salvation, they began to revere her as "the All-Holy", one who was "free from any stain of sin, as though fashioned by the Holy Spirit and formed as a new creature".[2] The fourth-century Saint Cyril of Jerusalem, for example, noted how the Holy Spirit "sanctified her, so as to enable her to receive Him through whom all things were made."[3] Saint Ephraim

[2] *CCC* 493, quoting Vatican II, Dogmatic Constitution on the Church, *Lumen Gentium*, November 21, 1964, no. 56.

[3] Cyril of Jerusalem, *Catecheses*, 17, 6: *PG* 33, 976.

(c. A.D. 350) called her "most holy, all-pure, all-immaculate, all stainless, all-undefiled."[4] Bishop Theoteknos of Livas in Palestine (c. A.D. 550–650) honored her as "holy and all-fair", "pure and stainless", and said, "She is born like the cherubim, she who is a pure, immaculate clay."[5]

Didn't Mary Need Salvation?

Still, some may wonder how Mary could be redeemed if she was immaculately conceived. This is a good question, one with which many theologians had wrestled in the Middle Ages. Christ died for all of mankind, to save us from sin. If Mary was preserved from original sin, then how could Christ be said to have died for all of Adam's descendants? It was the fourteenth-century theologian Blessed John Duns Scotus who best explained this aspect of the doctrine.[6] Scotus underscored how Mary is still a descendant of Adam in need of Christ's work of redemption, like the rest of us. But God, who is outside of time and space, could apply the saving fruits of Christ's death and Resurrection to Mary in a way that transcends ordinary time. He could bestow his redemptive grace on Mary at the moment of her conception, *preserving* her from the stain of original sin.

Mary was still completely dependent on God's saving grace, just as we are. The key difference is that while we receive this saving grace after we enter the world with original sin, Mary

---

[4] St. Ephraim the Syrian, *Precationes ad Deiparam* 1–2, in *Enchiridion Marianum biblicum patristicum*, ed. Dominici Casagrande (Rome: Cor Unum, 1974).

[5] Bishop Theoteknos of Livas in Palestine, Panegyric for the Feast of the Assumption, 5–6, in John Paul II, *Theotokos* (Boston: Pauline Books and Media, 1998), 91.

[6] Duns Scotus, *Lectura in Librum Tertium Sententiarum*.

From the *Symbolon* series

Coronation of Mary by Giulio Romano & Giovanni Francesco Penni (mosaic copy at St. Paul Outside the Walls, Rome)

received this grace in a preventative way. At the moment she was brought into existence in her mother's womb, she was filled with God's grace and persevered from original sin. As Saint John Paul II once said, "Mary was redeemed in an even more wonderful way, not by being freed from sin, but by being preserved from sin."[7] And with this unique grace, Mary stayed faithful to this gift, remaining free from sin for the whole of her life (see *CCC* 493).

[7]John Paul II, "General Audience", June 5, 1996, in *Theotokos*, 99.

The Virgin Mother: Mother of God
and Ever Virgin

A second Marian dogma is the divine maternity: Mary is the Mother of God. Like the other beliefs about Mary, her title Mother of God helps us understand who Jesus is. It tells us that her Child who took on her flesh was "the Father's eternal Son, the second person of the Holy Trinity", who is God himself (*CCC* 495). Since Jesus is true God and true man in the unity of his divine Person, to say Mary is not the Mother of God is to deny Christ's very divinity. Hence, it is important to hold that Mary is truly the Mother of God.

A third Marian doctrine is Mary's perpetual virginity. From the very beginning, the Church confessed that Mary conceived of Jesus as a virgin by the power of the Holy Spirit. We continue to proclaim this in the Creed when we say that Jesus "was conceived by the Holy Spirit, born of the virgin Mary". The virginal motherhood of Mary highlights how Jesus is truly human and truly divine. As a virgin, Mary conceives of Jesus purely by the power of the Holy Spirit, which points to Jesus' divine origins. But Mary is truly Christ's Mother, giving Jesus human flesh in her womb. The virginal conception is a sign that "it truly was the Son of God who came in a humanity like our own" (*CCC* 496).

As the Church deepened her appreciation for Mary's virginal motherhood, she also confessed Mary as remaining perpetually a virgin, for the rest of her life. Hence, the doctrine proclaims Mary as conceiving her Son as a virgin, giving birth to him as a virgin, and remaining a virgin for all of her life. Mary's perpetual virginity is important because it is an outward sign of her total faith and undivided gift of herself to her Son's mission, pointing to the kind of union with God to which we are all called (see *CCC* 506).

Jesus' Brothers?

Some, however, may wonder how Mary could have been a virgin throughout her life if the Bible clearly states that Jesus had brothers (see Mt 13:55). At first glance, these passages seem to contradict the Catholic belief in Mary's perpetual virginity. But on closer examination, we'll see that they actually support it.

First, since there was no word in Hebrew for "cousin", the Jews commonly used the word "brother" to describe cousins or other relatives. We can see this in the Greek Old Testament (the Septuagint), where the Greek word for brother—*adelphos*—is often used to describe relationships that go beyond actual brothers by blood. *Adelphos* could refer to an uncle (see Gen 13:8), a cousin (see 1 Chron 23:21–22), and even men from different families who were united together by a covenant (see 2 Sam 1:26). Hence, when the New Testament mentions the "brothers"—*adelphoi*—of Jesus, we should not assume that the term is pointing to actual physical brothers. The word could be referring to extended family members or others joined to him by covenant.

That, in fact, seems to be the case in Matthew 13:55, where two of the names of Christ's brothers (*adelphoi*) are given: James and Joseph. These "brothers" actually seem to be identified later in Matthew's Gospel as sons of a different Mary. At the cross, James and Joseph are mentioned as the sons of a woman named "Mary of Clopas", not the Blessed

Virgin Mary (see Mt 27:56). This, in fact, is how the *Catechism* explains it: "James and Joseph, 'brothers of Jesus,' are the sons of another Mary, a disciple of Christ whom St. Matthew significantly calls 'the other Mary' (*Mt* 13:55; 28:1; cf. *Mt* 27:56). They were close relations of Jesus, according to an Old Testament expression" (*CCC* 500).

This view is consistent with John's account of Christ's Passion, where Jesus entrusts his Mother into the care of the beloved disciple John. This is not something Jesus would do if he had natural brothers and sisters who could look after his Mother, Mary (see Jn 19:25–27). Think about how shocking this would be if Christ had blood brothers and sisters. Imagine Jesus telling his siblings, "My friend John— not you—is going to take care of Mom after I die." Most of the Church Fathers who commented on this question understood the brothers of Jesus not as natural siblings but as extended family members, born of a different mother (see *CCC* 500).

Assumption

The fourth key doctrine related to Mary is her Assumption. The Church teaches that, at the end of her earthly life, Mary, who was preserved free from original sin, was given the unique privilege of being assumed body and soul into heaven, anticipating the resurrection of all Christ's faithful at the end of time (see *CCC* 966, 974).

Three points stand out here. First, in discussing the Assumption, the Church mentions the idea of Mary's Immaculate Conception. If Mary was free from original sin, it is fitting that she, like her Son, would be spared one of the consequences of original sin, namely, the corruption of the body. Mary's body didn't face the same fate as the rest of the sons and daughters of Adam, who "are dust, and to dust [they] shall return" (Gen 3:19). Hence, the Church professes that Mary was taken into heaven, body and soul.

Second, the Church does not declare definitely whether Mary died and then was assumed into heaven or whether she was assumed without experiencing death. It leaves open both possibilities, simply stating that at the end of her earthly life she was taken body and soul into heaven. However, the majority of theologians and saints have concluded that Mary did in fact experience death, not as a punishment for sin, but in unity with her Son, who willingly experienced death on our behalf. This view also brings Mary in closer union with us. It's fitting that she who will pray for us "at the hour of our death" (as we say in the Hail Mary prayer) had experienced death herself.

Thirdly, while Mary's Assumption is a unique privilege, it should not be seen as detached from our own lives—a special grace given to Mary that we can admire from afar, but not something to which we can at all relate. Mary's Assumption stands as an "eschatological sign", a sign pointing to what God wants to accomplish in all of our lives. The New Testament makes it clear that all faithful disciples will share in Christ's glorious Resurrection, his victory over death. Since Mary is the first model disciple of Christ, it's fitting that she is the first to receive this blessing. She goes before us, experiencing the glorification of her body at the moment her earthly life ended. But her Assumption anticipates our own share in Christ's victory over death at the end of time in the resurrection of the body—if we persevere in faith like Mary did.

* * * * *

"Behold, your mother!" (Jn 19:27). These sacred words from the cross that Jesus spoke to the beloved disciple some two thousand years ago echo through the centuries and are spoken to us, the beloved disciples of Jesus, today. It's as if Jesus is tenderly speaking those words to you and me, inviting us to accept this gift of his Mother and welcome her into our lives. Will you see Mary as a model of faith that you should imitate? Will you trust that Mary, as your spiritual mother, loves you and prays for you? Will you welcome Christ's gift of his Mother in your life? How would you respond to Jesus saying to you, "Behold, your mother"?

Chapter Nine

The Last Things

What Happens After We Die?

Imagine your last moments on earth. It's shortly before you die, and a priest comes to give you a final blessing. He prays the following prayer over you, a prayer that might represent the last words you hear before entering eternity:

> Go forth, Christian soul, from this world
> In the name of God the almighty Father, who
>   created you,
> In the name of Jesus Christ, the Son of the living
>   God, who suffered for you,
> In the name of the Holy Spirit, who was poured
>   out upon you.
> Go forth, faithful Christian!

This traditional Catholic prayer known as the "Prayer of Commendation" is, in a sense, a traveler's prayer, entrusting the soul to God as it journeys to its eternal home. It goes on to say,

> May you live in peace this day.
> May your home be with God in Zion,

The Good Shepherd, Catacombs of St. Calixtus, Rome

> With Mary, the Virgin Mother of God,
> With Joseph, and all the angels and saints.

And it culminates with the hope that all the angels and saints will joyously welcome the soul into their communion of life and love with God in heaven.

> May you return to [your Creator]
> Who formed you from the dust of the earth.
> May holy Mary, the angels and all the saints
> Come to meet you as you go forth from this life....
> May you see your redeemer face to face.

Seeing God face-to-face is the goal of the Christian life. But what are the last things a soul may experience on its journey toward God in heaven? Here are some of the key questions we'll consider in this chapter:

- First, Christians say that, when we die, we all will go before the judgment seat of God. But on what will we be judged? And what are the consequences of this judgment?

- Second, we're going to look at the topic of hell. Is there really a hell? And if God is loving and merciful, does he really send some people to hell?
- Third, what is heaven? Heaven is supposed to be the goal of the Christian life, but if you ask a Christian what heaven is, many aren't sure what to say. We might have images of angels, harps, and clouds, but what exactly is heaven?
- Fourth, we're going to look at a commonly misunderstood Catholic belief about life after death: purgatory. Is purgatory a place where God inflicts his wrath on us until his anger is appeased? Is it an eternal middle zone between heaven and hell for those who were not good enough for heaven but were not bad enough for hell? Is it a second chance for those who didn't get it right in this life? We're going to consider what the Church really teaches about purgatory—and why.

Life After Death

What happens after we die? An inscription found on many ancient Roman tombstones sums up one popular view of death at the time: "I was not. I was. I am not. I do not care." In this perspective, there is nothing more to life than this world. There is no life after death. Death is a final end.

But the early Christians had a different view of death: death as a birth into new life. This can be seen in the title they gave their burial places. While the Romans typically called a burial site a "necropolis"—meaning "city of the dead"—the Christians gave their burial places a more hope-filled name. They called them "cemeteries", meaning sleeping rooms or resting places. The term reflected the distinctively Christian belief in the afterlife. Christians buried there were said to be simply "asleep" in Christ, awaiting the resurrection of their bodies. The Christians were so convinced of this that they decorated their burial places with many images that expressed this hope in the resurrection. For example, if you were to visit the ancient Christian underground cemeteries around Rome known as the "catacombs", you'd probably see several depictions of a good shepherd carrying a lamb on his shoulders, symbolizing how Jesus brings faithful Christians to their eternal rest in heaven. You'd also see images of an anchor, a biblical symbol for hope; a dove with an olive branch, symbolizing the soul resting in eternal peace; and a ship at sea, expressing the Christian journeying to the port of salvation. All these images make one thing clear: for the Christians, death was not a final end, but a passageway to eternal life.

Now, let's turn our attention to that ultimate threshold itself: What happens when we die?

Judgment

"Death" is the end of earthly life. But the soul is immortal; it lives forever. At the moment of bodily death, however, the soul is separated from the body. As Saint Paul said, "[W]e would rather be away from the body and at home with the Lord" (2 Cor 5:8).

When we die, we immediately go before God to be judged for the choices we made on earth. With death, "our life-choice becomes definitive—our life stands before the judge."[1] At the center of this judgment is the consideration of

[1] Benedict XVI, *Spe Salvi*, November 30, 2007, no. 45.

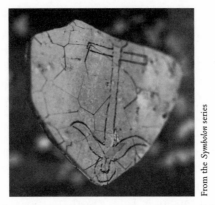

From the *Symbolon* series

Reproduction of Anchor Inscription in Catacombs of St. Calixtus, Rome

how well we loved God and neighbor. As Saint John of the Cross once said, "At the evening of life, we shall be judged on our love".[2] Those who die in friendship with God and in his grace are found worthy of heaven, whereas those who die outside of friendship with God and his grace will enter eternal separation from God: hell. The divine Judge doesn't make someone guilty or innocent. In his presence we will see ourselves as we really are. His judgment will declare us to be who we will have made ourselves out to be: either friends of God and worthy of heaven or among those who reject Christ and worthy of hell.

Heaven and Hell

There can be some people who, when they die, are already "perfectly purified" (*CCC* 1023). Their hearts have been

[2] *CCC* 1022, quoting St. John of the Cross, *Dichos* 64.

fully transformed by God's love. These people are "completely permeated by God and thus fully open to their neighbors—people for whom communion with God even now gives direction to their entire being and whose journey towards God only brings to fulfillment what they already are".[3] These souls go immediately to God when they die, and they will see God as he is. This life of perfect union with God is called heaven. As a share in the communion of life and love of the Holy Trinity with all the angels and saints, heaven is the fulfillment of our deepest longings, the perfection of happiness.

We cannot, however, possess this perfect union with God "unless we freely choose to love him" (*CCC* 1033). And we cannot love God if we sin gravely against him. There can be souls, therefore, who die outside of friendship with God, souls who have "totally destroyed their desire for truth and readiness to love, people for whom everything has become a lie, people who have lived for hatred and have suppressed all love within themselves".[4] Such souls remain separated from God forever by their own free choice. This definitive self-exclusion from God is called hell. The chief punishment in hell is eternal separation from the God in whom alone we can find the happiness we were made for.

But some may object, "How can a loving, merciful God send people to hell?" Here, it's important to emphasize that God does not predestine anyone to hell. But he does respect our freedom. He gave us free will so that we could love, so that we could freely choose to make our lives a gift to him. If a man, however, willfully turns away from God (through serious sin) and refuses to turn back and receive God's mercy,

---

[3] Benedict XVI, *Spe Salvi*, no. 45.
[4] Ibid., no. 45.

he freely chooses to separate himself from God forever. In this sense, hell is the ultimate working out of a person's having persistently pushed God out of his life on earth. Such a person, in the end, gets what he pursued during his time in this world: a life separated from God. So it is in this sense that we can say that God doesn't send anyone to hell, but some people, through their refusal to love, freely choose to go there.

Purgatory?

What happens to people who die in friendship with God, but their hearts are not totally for him? They have not yet been perfectly purified from their sins, attachments, willfulness, and self-love. They are not ready for complete union with the God of total, self-giving love.

Pope Benedict XVI taught that, presumably, for the great majority of people "there remains in the depths of their being an ultimate interior openness to truth, to love, to God. In the concrete choices of life, however, it is covered over by ever new compromises with evil—much filth covers purity, but the thirst for purity remains."[5] Such souls have a relationship with God, a genuine thirst for God, and will not be eternally separated from him. But at the same time, they are not ready for full communion with God. Remember, heaven is the perfect sharing in the total self-giving love of the Trinity. There's no one in heaven loving God with only half of his heart, 80 percent of his heart, or even 99.9 percent of his heart. In heaven, souls give themselves completely to God in love, 100 percent, holding nothing back.

[5] Ibid., no. 46.

So when souls die in friendship with God, but their hearts are still tainted by selfishness and pride, they are not ready for the total love of God in heaven. They need to be purified. This state of final purification after death is called purgatory. Souls in purgatory are assured of heaven, but they need to be purified before they can fully participate in the total love of the Trinity.

Saved through Fire

We can see a hint of purgatory in the Bible when Jesus alludes to the possibility of certain offenses being forgiven, not just in this age, but also "in the age to come" (Mt 12:32; see *CCC* 1031). Such forgiveness of sins in the age to come would not relate to souls in hell, who are eternally separated from God. Nor would it apply to the saints in heaven, who already have had their sins dealt with and now see God face-to-face. So the possibility of sins being forgiven not in this age but in the age to come must relate to a third state in which souls after death can be purified and forgiven. Catholics have called this third possible state after death "purgatory".

An even stronger biblical text pointing to purgatory is in Saint Paul's First Letter to the Corinthians. There, Paul speaks of souls who will be saved, but only "through fire" (1 Cor 3:15).

In the context leading up to this verse, Paul says that the foundation of the Christian life is Jesus Christ. As long as we build our lives on this foundation, nothing can take it away from us, even when we die. Paul notes, however, that individual Christians will be judged according to their works—according to how well they build from this foundation. Some will build their lives from this foundation well, using gold, silver, and precious stones, whereas other Christians, while remaining on the foundation of Christ, will not build well. Their works are only hay and straw.

> Now if any one builds on the foundation with gold, silver, precious stones, wood, hay, straw—each man's work will become manifest; for the day will disclose it, because it will be revealed with fire, and the fire will test what sort of work each one has done. If the work which any man has built on the foundation survives, he will receive a reward. If any man's work is burned up, he will suffer loss, though he himself will be saved, *but only as through fire.* (1 Cor 3:12–15; emphasis added)

Here we come to a key biblical image that can shed much light on what Catholics really believe about purgatory. In the last sentence of this passage, Saint Paul describes some souls who *"will be saved"* when the day of their judgment comes. First, note the word "saved": the souls described here are not condemned to hell, for they will one day experience salvation. But also notice the words "will be": these souls are not among the saints who immediately go to God in heaven, for Paul indicates their salvation is still in the future. They *"will* be saved". Saint Paul is alluding to some third state. And Paul describes what souls will experience in this state on their way to heaven: they will be saved, but "only as through fire". This fiery purification on the way to full union with God is what the Church calls "purgatory".

In the Catholic tradition, purgatory is sometimes associated with fire. But we shouldn't think of this fire in a purely negative sense, as if God has a need to inflict pain on us before letting us into his heavenly kingdom, baking us in a fiery furnace for hundreds of years until his anger is appeased. While in the Bible fire is sometimes associated with God's

Reproduction of Dove Inscription in Catacombs of St. Calixtus, Rome

From the *Symbolon* series

judgment and punishment, it also is a biblical image for his loving presence. At Pentecost, the Holy Spirit comes down on the apostles, and "there appeared to them tongues as of fire" (Acts 2:3). In the Exodus story, the Lord guides Israel through the desert with a pillar of fire, a symbol of God's holy presence in their midst. God reveals himself to Moses in the burning bush, where his holy presence was manifested in the form of fire. The book of Hebrews even calls God "a consuming fire" (Heb 12:29).

So fire can depict God's intimate, loving presence to his people. It is in this sense that we can see the saving fire of purgatory as God's love burning within us—transforming us, healing any vestiges of selfishness, and making us capable of perfect love. The burning flame of God's love liberates us from our self-centeredness and melts whatever aspects of our hearts are still hardened. "Purgatory is not ... some kind of supra-worldly concentration camp where man is forced to undergo punishment in a more or less arbitrary fashion. Rather is it the inwardly necessary process of transformation in which a person becomes capable of Christ, capable of God and thus capable of unity with the whole communion of saints."[6]

The Living Flame of Love

Such a transformation in a soul is beautiful—and painful. A helpful analogy for this reality can be found in Saint John of the Cross. The sixteenth-century mystic described how the Holy Spirit prepares a soul for ecstatic union with him, transforming the soul like fire consumes a log of wood. When a piece of wood becomes so penetrated by fire—so transformed by it and united with it—the wood flares up and blazes flames from itself. Similarly, when the soul is united with God, it is not just touched by the fire of his love. It is so inundated by the Holy Spirit that a living flame of divine love leaps up from within the soul itself. God's love is fully radiating through the soul, inspiring all of its actions.

But for souls who are not ready for this full encounter with God, the process is painful. For them, Saint John of the Cross says, the fire of God "is not gentle, but afflictive". The all-consuming divine love is experienced as a torment because the soul still resists God's love to some degree. The Holy Spirit "wounds the soul by destroying and consuming the imperfections of its bad habits" just as fire "makes an assault on a log of wood, wounding it with the flame, drying it out and stripping it of its unsightly qualities until it is so disposed that it can be penetrated and transformed into fire".[7]

[6]Joseph Ratzinger, *Eschatology* (Washington, D.C.: Catholic University Press, 1988), 230.

[7]St. John of the Cross, *The Living Flame of Love*, in *The Collected Works of Saint John of the Cross* (Washington, D.C.: ICS Publications, 1991), 1.19, p. 648.

In the fire of God's love, the soul experiences the pain of self-knowledge. Hidden weaknesses come into the open. The soul comes to terms with the depths of its selfishness, and it feels the full weight of its own inability to love completely. "All the soul's infirmities are brought to light; they are set before its eyes to be felt and healed.... It sees and feels those weaknesses and miseries that previously resided within it, hidden and unfelt, just as the dampness of the log of wood was unknown until the fire applied to it made it sweat and smoke and sputter."[8]

Saint John of the Cross used the fire and wood analogy to describe the intense spiritual purification some souls on earth might experience in the deeper stages of the spiritual life. But his imagery could just as well depict the souls in purgatory.[9] Their suffering entails a painful longing to be fully one with the God for whom they were made and a sorrow over their weaknesses that so clearly prevent them from doing so.

This is a point Pope Benedict XVI made. He taught that the purgatorial fire is actually a humbling, purifying encounter with Christ himself: "Before his gaze all falsehood melts away. This encounter with him, as it burns us, transforms and frees us.... All that we build during our lives can prove to be mere straw, pure bluster, and it collapses. Yet in the pain of this encounter, when the impurity and sickness of our lives become evident to us, there lies salvation. His gaze, the touch of his heart heals us through an undeniably painful transformation 'as through fire'."[10]

---

[8] Ibid., 1.21, p. 689.

[9] St. John of the Cross himself said these sufferings that a soul in the dark night endures are "little less than the sufferings of purgatory" (ibid., 1.21, p. 649).

[10] Benedict XVI, *Spe Salvi*, no. 47.

Shutterstock

Catacombs of St. Calixtus, Rome

Finally, the purification of souls on the way to heaven underscores the relationship between God's justice and mercy. On one hand, we see that how we choose to live matters and will have an effect not just in this world but also in our life after death. Pope Benedict asks what will happen to the souls who loved the Lord, but also covered themselves with impurity. What will happen when they go before the judgment seat of God? "Will all the impurity they have amassed through life suddenly cease to matter?"[11] Surely, our sins are not overlooked. They have real consequences that must be dealt with, for our own good, because they do damage to our souls. We must be healed of our patterns of self-love before we can enter full union with God.

On the other hand, we see in the reality of purgatory that our sins do not have to stain us forever. If we continue to

[11] Ibid., no. 46.

"reach out towards Christ, towards truth and towards love",[12] Christ can forgive and heal us, so that we might be disposed for full union with God. And he can do this purifying work in us during our life on earth and in the age to come, in purgatory.

Praying for the Dead

Christians have a responsibility to pray for their brothers and sisters in purgatory. This tradition of praying for the dead goes back to the ancient Jews and the early Church. In the Old Testament, Judas Maccabeus, for example, prayed for the dead, believing that prayers could make a difference for deceased souls, "that they might be delivered from their sin" (2 Mac 12:45). Similarly the early Christians offered prayers, sacrifices, penances, alms, and, above all, the Mass for souls to be purified, so that they might see God.

At the basis of this practice is the Christian conviction that "love can reach into the afterlife."[13] Our Christian brothers and sisters who have gone before us are not separated from us by death. The saints in heaven, the souls in purgatory, and the believers who are part of the pilgrim people of God on earth together form one Church and are united in one Lord, Jesus Christ. For the disciples of Christ, death does not cut off their relationship with the rest of the Church. An individual limb is not cut off from the body of Christ at death. Nor is a particular branch cut off from the vine. Hence, our prayers for each other bear fruit. Out of love for our brothers and sisters in purgatory, we should offer

[12] Ibid., no. 47.
[13] Ibid., no. 48.

prayers for them, confident that "our prayer is capable not only of helping them, but also of making their intercession for us effective" (*CCC* 958). "Even when they have crossed over the threshold of the world beyond, human beings can still carry each other and bear each other's burdens. They can still give to each other, suffer for each other, and receive from each other."[14] This intercession for each other builds up love in the body of Christ. Just as loving our neighbor on earth helps us grow in love for Christ our Lord, so also fellowship with our brothers and sisters in purgatory deepens our union with Christ himself.

The Last Judgment

Finally, let's consider the dramatic line from the Creed about what will happen at the end of time: "He will come again in glory to judge the living and the dead." This line refers to the final judgment, when Christ will come at the end of time to gather all nations and separate one from another like a shepherd separates the sheep from the goats (cf. Mt 25).

This is different from the particular judgment that each person faces when he dies. At death, the soul goes immediately to heaven, hell, or purgatory. But at the Last Judgment, the soul is reunited with the body in the resurrection of the dead. Those who have done good experience the resurrection of life, whereas those who have done evil face the resurrection of judgment (see *CCC* 1038).

At this climactic moment, the truth of each man's relationship with God is made known, and all the consequences of one's choices are laid bare. We will see the "ripple effect"

---

[14] Ratzinger, *Eschatology*, 227.

in human history of how we lived our lives. We will see the effect of all the good one has brought into the world, and we will see the consequences of what each individual failed to do (see *CCC* 1039). Most of all, Christ will give the final word on the history of the world, and we will see how God's providence directed everything to its ultimate destination, even in the midst of much weakness and sin. We will see how God triumphs over evil, how God's love is stronger than death, and how God wrote straight with our crooked lines.

But the Last Judgment still challenges us to take responsibility for our lives. Do we consider how our choices today affect our eternity? Do we embrace the role God calls us to play in our families, our communities, and the world around us? At the end of time, the story of our lives will have been definitively written and made known. How well will we have played our part? Death reminds us that we only have a short time to shape our life stories, to bring our lives to fulfillment, to make our lives something beautiful for God and the world.

Chapter Ten

Encountering Christ Today

The Seven Sacraments

Imagine being someone in ancient Rome wanting to convert to Christianity. After a long period of spiritual preparation, you would go to a sacred building called a "baptistry", and there, you would present yourself to be baptized by the bishop of Rome, the pope.

This would have been the most important moment in your life. You are about to be changed forever. You know that baptism cleanses the soul from sin and fills it with Christ's divine life. The God of the universe is about to come down and dwell within you through the grace of baptism!

As you enter the sacred building, practically everything you would do there would remind you of the spiritual transformation you are about to undergo. All the symbols and rituals from the ancient baptismal ceremony expressed the important step you were taking by turning away from sin and being joined to Christ.

Near the start of the ceremony, you would face west and say a prayer renouncing Satan and all his works. And then you would turn around and face east toward the baptismal font— where an action would soon take place that would symbolize

The Lateran Baptistry, Rome

the dawn of a new day in your life. The light of the world would soon fill your soul. You are turning around spiritually, turning away from sin, and taking on a new identity in Christ.

Then you would step into a large basin of water called the baptismal font, which was shaped like a Roman tomb. Stepping into this tomb-shaped basin symbolized how your baptism was a kind of death, a death to former ways of living, a death to sin, a death to your old self.

While you are in the water, the bishop would then ask you three questions based on the Creed: "Do you believe in God the Father Almighty ...? Do you believe in our Lord Jesus Christ, the Son of God ...? Do you believe in the Holy Spirit, the holy Catholic Church ...?" With each question, you would respond, "I believe", and be immersed in the water. You are being cleansed from sin as you are baptized into Christ.

Then you would rise out of the tomb-shaped baptismal font, symbolizing your resurrection to new life in Christ, and you would be dressed in white garments, pointing to how you have been purified from sin. Indeed, you are now clothed with the life of Christ, or in the words of Saint Paul, you have now "put on" (Gal 3:27) Christ.

All these and other rituals were meant to underscore how important the moment of baptism is for the Christian. The visible symbols expressed the profound invisible realities taking place in the soul when a person is baptized. Yet, baptism is just one of seven particular sacred rituals that Jesus Christ established to carry out his work of salvation in us— to forgive our sins, fill us with his life, and strengthen us in our journey of faith. Those seven sacred rites are called the sacraments.

What Are Sacraments?

Jesus died almost two thousand years ago. But how do we, today, receive what he won for us on the cross? All of mankind isn't automatically cleansed of sin and suddenly made holy just because Good Friday and Easter happened. Christ's redemptive work still has to be applied to our individual lives. But how does this occur? How do we access the "powers that come forth" from Christ's work of salvation? The short answer is, through the sacraments (see *CCC* 1116).

Catholics are known for going to Mass, confessing their sins to a priest, baptizing their babies, and getting married in the Church. But we shouldn't think of the sacraments merely as Catholic customs—rituals we go through just because we happen to be Catholic. Rather, the sacraments are God's way of infusing us with his life, the main "channels" he set up for imparting his grace to us so that we can become more like Christ and grow in deeper union with him.

Think of the sacraments as profound moments of encounter with the living Jesus. The Jesus who comforted and healed the suffering, who called people to repentance and forgave their sins, who promised to be with us and even abide *in* us—that living Jesus meets us through his grace in the sacraments. It's primarily through the sacraments that he pours his life into us to transform us, to make us more and more like him.

Does God Need All of This Ritual from Us?

According to a traditional textbook explanation, a sacrament is "an outward sign instituted by Christ to confer grace". There's a lot in this statement. Let's unpack what it means.

First, sacraments involve various *outward signs*—prayers, rituals, and material things such as bread, wine, candles, water, and oil, as well as a bishop, priest, or deacon leading the celebration. In essence, a sacrament has two main parts: physical elements and ritual words. In baptism, for example, the essential physical element is water and the essential words are the following: "I baptize you in the name of the Father, and of the Son, and of the Holy Spirit" (see Mt 28:19). In the Eucharist, the physical elements are bread and wine, and the words are the words of Christ spoken at the Last Supper and repeated at Mass by the priest: "This is my body.... This is my blood."[1]

Some, however, may wonder whether all this ritual is really necessary: "This is too complicated. I believe God is

---

[1] Mt 26:26, 28; Mk 14:22, 24; Lk 22:19; 1 Cor 11:24; see Lk 22:20; 1 Cor 11:25.

The Lateran Baptistry, Rome

much simpler than all this. Why do I need sacraments? God doesn't need bread and wine, water and oil to draw near to us. He doesn't need us to perform some rituals or need a priest to say some magical words."

It's true that God doesn't need all of this ritual ceremony. He's God and can impart his grace to us however he pleases. But *we* need ritual. And that's why God chose to encounter us in the sacraments.

God made us, and he knows how we work. Since we come to know reality through the senses, God uses various sights, sounds, movements—physical things, human instruments, and human words—to point to the profound spiritual realities we encounter when we receive his grace. The rituals of the sacraments are meant to grab our attention and wake us up, so that we can see with the eyes of the angels what's really happening when God imparts his life to us. God wisely uses what is visible, so that we can "see" the invisible. And he uses ceremony to express what words alone could never do. Through what is seen, heard, tasted, felt, and smelled, we become more aware of what is beyond the senses: the presence of Christ working in us through the sacraments.

Let's recall what happens at baptism, for example. Though various aspects of the baptismal celebration vary from time and place, the core, essential elements remain the same throughout the centuries. We saw in the early Roman Church how the *ritual washing* symbolizes the spiritual cleansing taking place within the soul. And we saw how the *emergence from the water* points to the soul now sharing in Christ's Resurrection, and the *white garment* symbolizes the soul, which is now clothed in his grace (see Rom 6:17). Other elements include a *candle*, which is lit to signify that Jesus is "the light of the world" and now shines in this soul. And the person is *anointed with sacred oil*, symbolizing how his soul is marked by Christ and anointed to share in his mission. A prayer blessing the water recalls how the waters of baptism don't just symbolize a spiritual cleansing. They also commemorate the great events of salvation history that prefigure baptism: just as the Spirit hovered over the waters at creation, so God's Spirit overshadows the baptismal waters, making them "a wellspring of all holiness". Just as the waters of the great flood "brought an end to sin and a new beginning of goodness" for mankind, so baptism marks a death to sin and new life in Christ. And just as Israel in the Exodus crossed the waters of the Red Sea to escape slavery under the Egyptians, so the baptismal waters represent a "new exodus" as we are "set free" from the slavery to sin (see *CCC* 1217–22).

Notice how all the details—all the ritual actions and all the ritual words—are not random procedures. They each have meaning and help give us a spiritual vision into what's really happening when we encounter God's grace in the sacraments.

Instituted by Christ

Second, the sacraments were instituted by Christ. They are not human inventions. They represent the way Jesus intended to free us from sin and fill us with his divine life. The Church gradually recognized seven sacraments as tremendous gifts given to us by Jesus.

The mysteries of Christ's entire life are the foundations for the sacraments. All of his words and actions during his ministry anticipate the saving power of his death and Resurrection—power that he would unleash through his apostles and the sacraments in the Church (see *CCC* 1115). Indeed, Jesus gave the apostles the Holy Spirit and entrusted them with his power to sanctify the world: "As the Father has sent me, even so I send you" (Jn 20:21). He commissioned the apostles to baptize "all nations" (Mt 28:19). He told them to celebrate the Eucharist "in remembrance of me" (1 Cor 11:24–25). He gave them power to forgive sins: "If you forgive the sins of any, they are forgiven" (Jn 20:23).

This is why the apostles went on to celebrate the Lord's Supper, to baptize, to anoint the sick, to forgive people's sins, and to lay hands on deacons and successors who share in their ministry in the Church.[2] And this ministry has been handed on by the Holy Spirit to the apostles' successors throughout the centuries to the bishops, priests, and deacons who celebrate the sacraments today. It is in this way that Christ's work of salvation is passed on to the entire world, to the end of time, through the sacraments.

[2] See Jn 4:2; Acts 2:41; 6:3–6; 13:1–3; 20:7; 1 Cor 11:23–32; Mk 6:13; Jas 5:14–15; 2 Tim 1:6–7; 2:1–2.

The key to see here is that it is Christ himself working through the ordained ministers and the sacramental signs to impart his life to us. Indeed, as the *Catechism* explains, Jesus, who sits at the right hand of the Father in heaven, "now acts through the sacraments he instituted to communicate his grace" (*CCC* 1084).

Yet, some might wonder, "Can't God work on his own, apart from our human celebration of sacraments?" Sure. But the sacraments are the ordinary ways in which he imparts his grace to us. They are the ways he established, the ways he wants us to approach him. And they are the ways Christians have followed from the very beginning.

Still, some might object, saying, "I just want to go to God directly. I don't want to work with a priest. He's just a human being, after all—not God." Such an objection, however, is not in harmony with Scripture. Saint Paul teaches that Jesus is the "one" mediator between God and man (see 1 Tim 2:5) in the sense that Christ is the unique, primary mediator. All other mediation, whether it be through priests, the saints, or the Church, is only effective because it is based on Christ as the one, unique, foundational mediator between God and man.[3] But Paul is not excluding the mediation of himself as an apostle, of his fellow apostles, of the Church as a whole, or of any ministry as a channel of grace, "as long as it serves the mediation of Christ, which alone is sufficient".[4]

---

[3] As the *Catechism* explains, man's mediation, like that of Mary's, "in no way obscures or diminishes this unique mediation of Christ, but rather shows its power" (*CCC* 970, quoting Vatican II, Dogmatic Constitution on the Church, *Lumen Gentium*, November 21, 1964, no. 60). The fact that Christ can invite weak, sinful, fallible human beings into his plan of salvation and even use us as instruments of his grace shows how powerful his mediation is.

[4] G. Montague, *First and Second Timothy* (Grand Rapids, Mich.: Baker Academic, 2008), 56.

Door of the Sacraments, St. Peter's Basilica, Rome

That's why Paul himself spoke about cooperating in Christ's ministry of reconciliation (see 2 Cor 5:17–18). He described himself as a minister of God's word (see 1 Thess 2:13), interceding for his people (see Phil 1:4), and being appointed an apostle to the gentiles by God (see Rom 11:13). He also wrote about how Christians are called to be "God's fellow workers" (1 Cor 3:9), and how the Church is the "pillar and bulwark of the truth" (1 Tim 3:15) for God's people, making the manifold wisdom of God known even to the angels (see Eph 3:10).

All this makes sense. God has always used human leaders and institutions to establish and deepen his relationship with his people. In the Old Testament, God worked through Moses to part the Red Sea so that the Israelites could escape from the Egyptians. Imagine, however, if an Israelite said that day, "I don't want to work with Moses, Lord. I only want to work with you." Such a man would miss out on the saving work God was offering his people through Moses. Instead of being rescued that day, the man would have been captured by the Egyptians and kept in slavery.

Similarly, God worked through the prophet Elisha to cure a man named Namaan of his leprosy (see 2 Kings 5:1–14). But imagine if Namaan said, "Get away from me, Elijah. I want God to heal me directly." Namaan would have remained a leper, missing out on the amazing gift of healing God was offering him through Elisha.

Similarly, Jesus in the New Covenant offers the world amazing gifts of healing, forgiveness, and strength through the apostles and their successors today, the ordained ministers who celebrate the sacraments. Following the biblical pattern, Jesus employs human leaders as his instruments to carry out his saving plan. He gave the apostles authority to teach and heal in his name and charged them to continue his mission of forgiving sins and imparting his life to the world (see Mt 10:1–8). Jesus viewed himself as working so powerfully through the apostles that he said to them, "He who hears you hears me, and he who rejects you rejects me" (Lk 10:16). We don't want to be among those who willfully reject God's appointed human instruments and thus miss out on the wonderful gifts of salvation Christ offers us through the sacraments.

To Confer Grace

We've seen how the sacraments involve outward signs that point to an interior grace. Now, we'll consider how they do more—much more. Sacraments actually effect, bring about, what they signify.

This is truly amazing. The sacraments of Christ have the power to make present the graces they signify. Sacramental signs are thus different from any other sign in the world. A red stoplight at an intersection, for example, indicates that a car should stop at that point. But the red light does not have the power to make cars come to a halt. Drivers can still choose to go through the intersection. A sacramental sign, however, doesn't just point to what should be happening. It actually conveys the grace that it signifies. The waters of baptism, for example, don't just symbolize the importance of spiritual cleansing. Through the ritual cleansing of the sacrament itself, God really makes the person's soul clean. Similarly, the bread and wine used at Mass don't just symbolize spiritual nourishment; they are changed into Christ's Body and Blood and thus really feed the soul with Christ's presence.

So important are the graces of the sacraments for the Christian's life, that Jesus did not make them dependent on the holiness of the minister or the person receiving the sacrament. The sacraments are based on the power of God. According to a traditional Latin expression, the sacraments act *ex opera operato*, literally "by the work worked", which means that Christ works with his saving power by the fact that the action has been performed. That's how much Christ loves us and wants to share his life with us! Whenever the sacraments are celebrated with the intent of the Church, Jesus is present with his grace. God's power is working through them, even if the minister of the sacrament is weak or sinful. As Saint Augustine once said, "When Peter baptizes it is Christ who baptizes. . . . When Judas baptizes, it is Christ who baptizes." He elsewhere made the point even more dramatically: "Those whom a drunkard baptized, those whom a murderer baptized, those whom an adulterer baptized, if it was the baptism of Christ, were baptized by Christ."[5]

[5] St. Augustine, *Tractates on the Gospel of John*, 6 and 5:18, Nicene and Post-Nicene Fathers, series 1, vol. 7. See also Scott Hahn, *Swear to God: The Promise and Power of the Sacraments* (New York: Doubleday, 2004), 19.

But this doesn't mean the sacraments work like magic. They don't automatically make us holy. The impact a sacrament has in our lives depends on the dispositions we bring to them (see *CCC* 1128). The seeds of sacramental grace are sown, but how much they bear fruit in our lives depends on what kind of "soil" in our souls those seeds meet.

One great story from the Gospels that expresses this point is found in Luke's Gospel (8:42–48). While Jesus was traveling in Galilee, large crowds pressed around him. But one woman who had been suffering from a hemorrhage for twelve years came up from behind Jesus and reached out to touch the fringe of his garment. She was immediately healed. Jesus stopped at that moment and asked, "Who was it that touched me?" Everyone denied it, and Peter thought it was a strange question for Jesus to ask since there were so many in the crowd all around him, so he said, "Master, the multitudes surround you and press upon you!" (8:45). But Jesus was persistent. Someone made contact with him in a different way: "Someone touched me; for I perceive that power has gone forth from me" (8:46). Finally, the woman came forth trembling and fell before Jesus, explaining what she did and how she had been healed. Jesus praised her great faith and told her to go in peace. "Daughter, *your faith* has made you well" (8:48; emphasis added).

It's fascinating that when the *Catechism of the Catholic Church* describes the sacraments, it does so echoing language form this very story. Just as "power" had "gone forth" from Jesus that day to heal the hemorrhaging woman, so the *Catechism* says, "Sacraments are 'powers that comes [*sic*] forth' from the body of Christ [the Church]" (*CCC* 1116).

Here's the key connection: In the Gospel account, many people crowded around Jesus and made contact with him that day. But only one reached out with great faith, and she

The Jordan River

was healed. None of the others had a dramatic transformation, but the woman who came with faith did.

Similarly, some Catholics who come in contact with the real graces of the sacraments—they may go to Mass, receive confirmation, or get married in the Church—show few signs of spiritual growth. Is that because the sacraments aren't working? No. It could be because of a lack of faith—the lack of love, devotion, and trust we bring to the sacraments. As Scripture commentator Timothy Gray expressed, "How many Catholics go to Mass or receive Confirmation and nothing changes in their life? They are like the crowd that was very close to Jesus, but did not reach out to Him in faith."[6]

---

[6]Tim Gray, *Sacraments in Scripture* (Steubenville, Ohio: Emmaus Road, 2001), 25–26.

Yet, if we approach the sacraments like the woman with the hemorrhage approached Jesus, the graces of the sacrament will bear more fruit in our lives. This doesn't mean that we will automatically experience great miracles, healing, or overnight sanctification. But when our souls are well-disposed, their power is even more effective. That's why we must draw near to Jesus in the sacraments with humility, recognizing our need for his help. We must come with hearts full of love, longing for him to fill us with his grace. And we must come with faith, confident that he can help us, change us, and strengthen us to grow in the Christian life. When we come with the right dispositions, the graces imparted in the sacraments can change our lives.

Growing Up in God's Family

Christ encounters us in the sacraments at the critical moments in our lives. The seven sacraments can be seen as working together throughout one's journey of faith and corresponding to the different stages of one's personal life (see *CCC* 1210).

Baptism represents our *birth* into God's family. It's when we become children of God. Christ sends his Spirit into our hearts at baptism. We are filled with his divine life and are born anew as God's sons and daughters by grace.

Confirmation can be seen as *preparation for spiritual maturity* in God's family. Through this sacrament, the Holy Spirit unites us more fully to Christ and the Church's mission, increases the gifts of the Holy Spirit in us, and strengthens us to bear witness to Christ in the world. We as children of God are formed to participate in a more mature way in the mission of Christ's Church.

Christ also meets us when we enter *marriage*. The sacrament of matrimony elevates the couple's human love to participate in God's divine love, so that they can love and serve each other far beyond what they could do on their own. And in their grace-filled marriage, they now can serve as a profound sign of God's love in the world.

And Jesus comes to us near the *end* of our lives or when we face severe illness. In those moments of suffering or when we are preparing to enter eternal life, we need extra help. We need to be strengthened in the faith to help us persevere through those trials. This happens in the anointing of the sick.

But there are two other sacraments that correspond to particular needs we have all throughout our lives. Week after week we need *spiritual nourishment*. We need to be fed by Christ in the Eucharist, which is the covenant family meal. Nourished with the Body and Blood of Christ at Mass, we are continually filled with his life and strengthened to live ever more like the One whom we receive in Holy Communion.

But we also need to encounter *Christ's mercy* on a regular basis. Whenever we sin, whether in big or small matters, we hurt our relationship with God and others. We need a way to be reconciled with our heavenly Father and with the family of God. And we need the grace to help us improve, so that we can avoid sin in the future. That happens most powerfully in the sacrament of confession.

Finally, God's covenant family needs leaders to serve his people in teaching, celebrating the sacraments, and governance. That's why Christ appointed the twelve apostles to share in his mission. Holy orders is the sacrament through which Christ's mission entrusted to the apostles is carried out to the end of time. Through the laying on of hands from one bishop to the next, from one generation to the next, the apostolic mission is passed on throughout the centuries to the apostles' successors today—the bishops, priests, and deacons who participate in that apostolic mission by varying degrees.

This is the big picture of the sacraments in the Catholic Church. Now in the next few chapters, we turn our attention to the two sacraments that should be a regular part of every Catholic's spiritual life: the Eucharist and confession.

Chapter Eleven

The Holy Eucharist

God with Us

Love wants to be near the beloved. And the God who is love was so driven by his love for us that he actually became man and dwelt among us. He even died on the cross for us so that we would no longer be separated from him by our sin.

But in his love for us, God went another step further. He chose to remain near us in the Eucharist, really present under the signs of bread and wine. Think about that: the God who created the universe comes upon our altars at Mass and unites himself to us in a most intimate Holy Communion.

It's no wonder one of the first titles given to Jesus was "Emmanuel", which means "God with us". It's a name that refers not only to Jesus as the God who became man and dwelt among the Jewish people some two thousand years ago, but also to the Jesus who remains "God with us" even today in the gift of his Real Presence to us in the Eucharist.

But to appreciate the incredible gift of the Eucharist and experience its power in our lives, we must understand three key aspects of this sacrament: the Eucharist as Real Presence, as sacrifice, and as Holy Communion.

From the *Symbolon* series

The Last Supper, St. John Lateran, Rome

Real Presence

At every Mass, we remember how, on the night before he died, at the Last Supper, Jesus instituted the Eucharist. He took bread and said, "Take this, all of you, and eat of it, for this is my body." And he took a chalice of wine and said, "Take this, all of you, and drink from it, for this is the chalice of my blood."

But what did Jesus mean by this? Did he really intend for us to eat of his body and drink of his blood?

Jesus' presence in the Eucharist is different from other ways he is close to us. Jesus said he would be present to his people in many ways. He is present in prayer. "For where two or three are gathered in my name, there am I in the midst of them" (Mt 18:20). He is present in the Scriptures, the sacraments, and the priests. And he is present in the poor, sick, and imprisoned (see Mt 25:31–46).

Catholics, however, believe Jesus is uniquely present in the Eucharist. In this most Blessed Sacrament, Jesus is present in the fullest sense, making himself, as the *Catechism* expresses, "wholly and entirely present".[1] For the Eucharist is not just a symbol of Jesus or a sacred reminder of his love for us. The Eucharist, in a most profound sense, *is* Jesus. At the words of Consecration at Mass—when the priest repeats Jesus' words from the Last Supper, saying, "This is my body.... This is my blood"—the bread and wine are changed into Christ's Body, Blood, Soul, and Divinity.

But how can this be? Can a sliver of bread and a drop of wine really be changed into Jesus' Body and Blood? The Eucharist, after all, still looks, tastes, feels, and smells like bread and wine. How could one say that it's really Christ's Body and Blood if our senses tell us otherwise?

The theological term used to express this change is "transubstantiation" (meaning "change of substance"). The word describes how, while the appearances of bread and wine remain, "there takes place a change of the whole substance of the bread into the substance of the body of Christ our Lord and of the whole substance of the wine into the substance of his blood".[2]

It's important to note, however, that this is not a chemical change. If one were to put the eucharistic Host under a microscope, a divine gall bladder would not appear through the lens. Nor would one discover holy blood cells or supernatural hemoglobin when conducting scientific experiments on the eucharistic Blood of Christ. The Eucharist still looks, tastes, and feels like bread and wine, but underneath those outward sensory appearances, Christ's Body and Blood is really present (see *CCC* 1376). As one early Christian theologian, Saint Cyril of Jerusalem, expressed, "Do not see in the bread and wine merely natural elements, because the Lord

---

[1] *CCC* 1374, quoting Paul VI, *Mysterium Fidei*, September 3, 1965, no. 39.
[2] *CCC* 1376, quoting the Council of Trent (1551): DS 1642.

has expressly said they are his body and his blood: faith assures you of this, though your senses suggest otherwise."[3]

The Bible reveals how God's words are so powerful that whatever he commands is carried out. When he says, "Let there be light" (Gen 1:3), at creation, light suddenly appears. At his word, the sun, moon, and stars are brought into existence. The power of that divine word is also in Jesus. When Jesus tells a paralyzed man, "Rise, take up your pallet, and walk", the man is immediately healed and begins to walk (Jn 5:8–9). When Jesus tells the dead Lazarus to come out of the tomb, Lazarus comes out risen from the dead (see Jn 11:43–44). And when he tells a person "your sins are forgiven" (Mt 9:2), he is truly forgiven. Similarly, Jesus took bread and said, "This is my body", and took wine and said, "This is my blood" (Mt 26:26–28). These sacred words bring about what he says. Catholics believe that the same divine word in Christ that had the power to heal, raise people from the dead, and forgive sins can change bread and wine into his Body and Blood.

What Jesus Taught

This idea of the Real Presence of Jesus in the Eucharist is rooted in Christ's own teachings. When Jesus taught about the Eucharist, he spoke with a profound realism. At the Last Supper, he didn't say, "This is a *symbol* of my body." He said, "This *is* my body." And when he gave his most in-depth teaching on the Eucharist, he spoke in a very realistic way—in a way that makes clear that the Eucharist is not just a symbol of Jesus, but is his flesh and blood made sacramentally present.

Let's enter into that dramatic scene, known as the "Bread of Life Discourse" in John's Gospel, chapter 6. Jesus has just

[3] As quoted by John Paul II in *Ecclesia de Eucharisitia*, April 17, 2003, no. 15.

Church of the Gesù, interior, Rome

performed his greatest miracle so far, multiplying loaves and fish to feed five thousand people. The crowds are in awe. They declare him to be the great "prophet who is to come" and want to carry him off "to make him king" (Jn 6:14–15).

But the very next day, Jesus says something that sends his public approval ratings plummeting, something that makes those same raving fans now oppose him. Even some of his own disciples will walk away from him. What does Jesus say that's so controversial? He teaches about partaking of his Body and Blood in the Eucharist.

Jesus first says, "I am the bread of life ... come down from heaven" (Jn 6:35, 38). And he goes on to make clear that he is not speaking in some vague, metaphorical sense. He says, "[A]nd the bread which I shall give for the life of the world *is my flesh*" (Jn 6:51; emphasis added).

The people are shocked at this. They say, "How can this man give us his flesh to eat?" (Jn 6:52). Notice how the Jews listening that day don't take Jesus as speaking metaphorically, as if they are merely being told to eat of his flesh in some merely symbolic way. They understand Jesus very well. They know he is speaking realistically here, and that's why they are appalled.

Now here's the key: Jesus has every opportunity at this point to clarify his teaching if he sensed the people were misunderstanding him. In other words, if Jesus was only intending to speak about eating his flesh in a figurative way, he could quickly back up and say, "Wait ... I'm sorry.... You misunderstood me. I was just speaking metaphorically here!" He could have softened his teaching, saying. "Let me explain. You don't need to eat my flesh. You just need to nourish yourself on my teaching, my wisdom, my love." But this is exactly what Jesus does *not* do at this point. He uses even more graphic, more intense language to drive his point home about how we need to really partake of his flesh and blood: "Truly, truly, I say to you, unless you eat the flesh of the Son of man and drink his blood, you have no life in you" (Jn 6:53). And he goes on to underscore how essential partaking of his Body and Blood is for our salvation. "[H]e who eats my flesh and drinks my blood has eternal life, and I will raise him up at the last day. For my flesh is food indeed, and my blood is drink indeed. He who eats my flesh and drinks my blood abides in me, and I in him" (6:54–55).

This is not the language of someone speaking metaphorically. Jesus wants to give us his very Body and Blood in the Eucharist. In fact, he now uses a word for "eat" that has even greater graphic intensity—*trogein*, which means "to chew or gnaw"—not a word that would be used figuratively here!

So challenging is this teaching that even many of Christ's disciples are bewildered. They say, "This is a hard saying; who can listen to it?" (Jn 6:60). Indeed, Christ's words on the Eucharist were too much for some of them to believe. Many of his disciples rejected Jesus over this teaching and left him (see Jn 6:66). And Jesus let them go. He didn't chase after them, saying, "Wait! You misunderstood me!" They understood quite well that Jesus was talking about eating his flesh and blood, and they rejected his teaching. In fact, Jesus is so serious about wanting to be this intimately close to us in the Eucharist that he even turns to the twelve apostles at this point and says, "Will you also go away?" (Jn 6:67). The partaking of his Body and Blood is so important to Jesus that he makes this teaching a crucial test for being a true disciple. He wants his followers to trust him, even if they don't fully understand. Peter, probably just as uncertain as the others are as to how this can be, nevertheless trusts Jesus' words. He doesn't say, "Oh yes, Jesus. This all makes perfect sense to me." Rather, he responds in trusting faith, saying, "Lord, to whom shall we go? You have the words of eternal life" (Jn 6:68).

The Mass as Sacrifice

Another key aspect of the Eucharist and its power in our lives is that it is a sacrifice. In fact, the eucharistic celebration is often described as the Holy Sacrifice of the Mass.

In the Bible, however, the idea of sacrifice brings to mind priests offering up cattle, sheep, and goats in the temple, blood being poured out on the altar, and the body being consumed with fire. Nothing like that happens at the Catholic Mass! So how would the Mass be a sacrifice?

But the Mass does involve a true sacrifice—the sacrifice of Jesus Christ, who in his death offered his life as a total gift of love to the Father and brought about the salvation of

"Last Communion of St. Jerome" by Domenichino
(mosaic copy in St. Peter's Basilica, Vatican City)

From the *Symbolon* series

the world. The Catholic Church teaches that Mass doesn't just recall or symbolize this sacrifice of Christ. It actually makes it present so that the redeeming power of the cross might more deeply transform our lives. As the *Catechism of the Catholic Church* explains, "In this divine sacrifice which is celebrated in the Mass, the same Christ who offered himself once in a bloody manner on the altar of the cross is contained and offered in an unbloody manner".[4]

To understand how important this aspect of the Mass is for our lives, we need to consider how Jesus instituted the Eucharist in the context of a Passover meal, the greatest of Jewish festivals. It celebrated the first Passover in Egypt—that fateful night when God liberated Israel from slavery in Egypt

[4] *CCC* 1367, quoting the Council of Trent (1562): *Doctrina de ss. Missae sacrificio*, c. 2: DS 1743.

(see Ex 12:1–28). That's when God instructed the people to sacrifice a lamb, eat of it, and put the lamb's blood on their doorposts as a sign of their faithfulness. The households who did this were spared when all firstborn sons of Egypt were struck down in a severe plague. That night, Pharaoh finally gave the Israelites their freedom, and year after year the Israelites celebrated the Passover as a "memorial" (*anamnesis* in Greek) of this foundational event in their history (Ex 12:14).

In the annual Passover feast, the Israelites retold the story of the first Passover and reenacted it by eating a ritual meal with the sacrificed lamb as the main course. But they also did something more. As a liturgical "memorial", the celebration didn't just recall the past—it *relived* the past. The past event was here and now mystically made present to those participating in the meal. Jews in Jesus' day, in fact, believed that when they celebrated the Passover they were at one with their ancestors from the first Passover. As one Jewish rabbi later explained, "In every generation a man must so regard himself as if he came forth himself out of Egypt."[5] The *Catechism of the Catholic Church* expresses this point in a similar manner:

> In the sense of Sacred Scripture the *memorial* is not merely the recollection of past events but the proclamation of the mighty works wrought by God for men. In the liturgical celebration of these events, they become in a certain way present and real. This is how Israel understands its liberation from Egypt: every time Passover is celebrated, the Exodus events are made present to the memory of believers so that they may conform their lives to them (*CCC* 1363; emphasis in original).

[5] Pesahim 10, 5, in the *Mishnah*, trans. Herbert Danby (Oxford: Oxford University Press, 1933), 151.

It was in this way that the "memorial" of the Passover united God's people across the centuries. Later generations could participate with their ancestors in this foundational event of Israel's history. All were rescued from Egypt. All were united in God's covenant family.

The New Passover

Now, imagine being one of the apostles there at the Last Supper, at the great Passover meal when Jesus instituted the Eucharist.

One thing that would stand out to you is the sacrificial overtones of Jesus' words and actions—and how he applied those words and actions to himself. On a basic level, the mere fact that Jesus instituted the Eucharist during the Passover would be significant, because the Passover itself was a sacrificial feast (see Ex 12:27).

You would also notice how Jesus speaks of his body being "given up". This is technical language bringing to mind the idea of a sacrifice being "given up" to God. In fact, the particular word for "given up" in Luke's account of the Last Supper (*didomai* in Greek) is employed elsewhere in the New Testament in association with sacrifice (see Mk 10:45; Lk 2:24; Jn 6:51; Gal 1:4).

A third aspect of the Last Supper that would stand out to you is how Jesus speaks about his blood being "poured out ... for the forgiveness of sins" (Mt 26:28). This would recall the sacrifices in the temple where the blood of the animal is poured out over the altar so that sins might be forgiven (see Lev 4:7, 18, 25, 30, 34). Finally, when Jesus speaks of "my blood of the covenant" (Mt 26:28), he echoes what Moses said in the sacrificial ceremony at Mount Sinai when God

Remains of Synagogue in Capernaum, site of Jesus' Bread of Life discourse.

forged his covenant relationship with the people of Israel. In that scene, Moses took blood from the sacrificed animals and said, "Behold the blood of the covenant" (Ex 24:8). In like manner, Jesus took the chalice and spoke of *his* blood as "my blood of the new covenant". The connection between the two scenes is striking. Just as the Old Covenant was established with Moses and the sacrificial "blood of the covenant", so the New Covenant is being established with Jesus and the sacrificial "blood of the new covenant"—which is not the blood of some sacrificial animal, but Christ's.

So picture being a first-century Jew at the Last Supper encountering these many sacrificial themes all at once: a Passover meal, a body being "given up", blood being "poured out ... for the forgiveness of sins", and this blood being described as "the blood of the new covenant". All this would tell you that Jesus has some kind of sacrifice in mind. But the most important sacrifice at this meal is not what we would expect: it's not a sacrificial lamb that's central. Instead, Jesus puts *himself* at the center of this Passover sacrifice. It's *his* body being offered up. It's *his* blood that is being poured out. It's *his* blood that is the blood of the covenant.

Jesus associates himself with the Passover lamb, and in so doing, he sheds light on his imminent death on the cross. Jesus will die, not as a passive victim at the hands of the Romans; he will go to the cross voluntarily offering his life as a sacrifice for our salvation. Here at the Last Supper, Jesus willingly offers up his body and blood "for the forgiveness of sins", and this interior sacrifice will be carried out externally in his body the next day.[6]

"Do This in Memory of Me"

Now we come to the heart of the matter. This connection between the Last Supper and the Cross—between Christ's offering his Body and Blood in the Eucharist and his offering of his life on Calvary—is crucial for understanding the Mass as a sacrifice. For at the very end of the Last Supper meal, Jesus says, "Do this in remembrance of me" (Lk 22:14).

Two points stand out in this command. First, what is the "this" Jesus wants the apostles to do? He wants them to celebrate this sacrifice of the Last Supper, to offer this new

[6] "Jesus did not simply state that what he was giving them to eat and drink was his body and blood; he also expressed its *sacrificial meaning* and made sacramentally present his sacrifice which would soon be offered on the Cross for the salvation of all" (John Paul II, *Ecclesia de Eucharistia*, no. 12; emphasis in original).

Passover sacrifice of his body and blood. Second, in what manner are they to do this? As a biblical *memorial*. Jesus says, "Do this in remembrance of me." The word "remembrance" here, like the word "memory" used at Mass, translates the biblical word for "memorial", which we've seen means a lot more than recalling a past event. In the Bible, a liturgical memorial makes present the past event so that it can be relived by later generations. So when Jesus tells the apostles, "Do this in remembrance of me," he's not instructing them to celebrate a ritual that merely remembers Jesus or reenacts what he did at the Last Supper. Rather, he is commanding them to celebrate the Last Supper as a liturgical memorial— making present the whole reality of this sacred meal, most especially his sacrificial offering of his body and blood.

Indeed, the Eucharist is the new Passover meal. Just as the old Passover feast was a memorial making present the foundational event for God's people of old, so now the Eucharist is the new Passover making present the foundational event of the New Covenant: Christ's sacrifice on the cross. Through the regular celebration of the Eucharist, the events of the Last Supper and the Cross are sacramentally made present to us, so that we can unite our lives to them. As the *Catechism* explains, "When the Church celebrates the Eucharist, she commemorates Christ's Passover, and it is made present: the sacrifice Christ offered once for all on the cross remains ever present" (*CCC* 1364).

Christ makes his sacrifice present to us in the Mass so that its saving power may be applied more profoundly to our daily lives. In every Mass we are united to Christ's total, self-giving love on Calvary. We have the opportunity sacramentally to enter into that loving gift of himself to the Father. We unite all our prayers, works, joys, and sufferings of each day to

Christ's offering of himself in love to the Father. And as we share in Christ's perfect act of love on the cross, we grow in sacrificial love ourselves. For in the Mass, we encounter Love himself in the most profound way. By participating in the Mass and receiving him in Holy Communion, we welcome Christ to live out his sacrificial love ever more in us. "In the Eucharist the sacrifice of Christ becomes also the sacrifice of the members of his Body. The lives of the faithful, their praise, sufferings, prayer, and work, are united with those of Christ and with his total offering, and so acquire a new value. Christ's sacrifice present on the altar makes it possible for all generations of Christians to be united with his offering" (*CCC* 1368).

Holy Communion

In the Passover ritual, as in other Jewish sacrifices, it was not enough for the animal to be slayed. The lamb had to be eaten (see Ex 12:8–12). After the lamb was sacrificed, there was a communion meal, which was an essential part of the Passover and the climax of the ritual. Shared meals in the Bible symbolize a profound solidarity between two people, a new shared life. So it was the partaking of the sacrificial lamb that deepened covenant union between God and his people.

This has important ramifications for understanding a third aspect of the Eucharist, *Holy Communion.* The Bible reveals Jesus is the new Passover lamb offering himself in sacrifice for our sins.[7] So it would be fitting for there to be a communion meal associated with his sacrifice on Calvary. From a biblical

[7]See 1 Cor 5:7–8; 1 Pet 1:19; Rev 5:6.

perspective, the Passover lamb can't just be sacrificed. It has to be eaten! If, therefore, Jesus is the new Passover lamb, we might expect there to be a communion meal in which we partake of the lamb, Jesus Christ.

This is what Saint Paul seems to assume in his First Letter to the Corinthians. He writes, "Christ, our Paschal Lamb, has been sacrificed. Let us, therefore, celebrate the festival" (1 Cor 5:7–8). We see here how Paul views Christ's sacrifice as culminating in a festive meal. And he makes clear that the festive meal he has in mind is the Eucharist. Later in the letter he gives an account of how Jesus instituted the Eucharist at the Last Supper (see 1 Cor 11:23–26), and he describes the union we have with Christ and each other when we partake of the Eucharist (see 1 Cor 10:16–17). All this perfectly reflects the biblical pattern of sacrifice and communion.

Holy Communion, therefore, is the climax of our worship at Mass. The Mass is "wholly directed toward the intimate union of the faithful with Christ through communion. To receive communion is to receive Christ himself who has offered himself for us" (*CCC* 1382). When we receive the Eucharist, we are receiving Christ himself in the most profound union we can have with God here on earth!

Especially after receiving Communion, we want to give God our fullest love and attention. When we come back to our pews, our God is dwelling within us. This is not the time to look around and see what people are wearing or to develop our "parking lot exit strategy" for after Mass. And it's certainly not appropriate to leave early before Mass is over. This is the most important time in our lives to rest in God's presence and talk to him, heart-to-heart. As he lovingly dwells inside us, we should tell him we love him, express thanks to him for the blessings in our lives, and pour

Tabernacle, Basilica of St. Mary Major's, Rome

out our hearts to him—our needs, our fears, our hurts. If we don't take time to talk to God when we receive him in the Eucharist, when will we ever really talk to him? Especially in Holy Communion, Jesus wants to heal us of our weaknesses, strengthen us in his love, and change us to become more and more like him.

Making a Visit

Finally, we see how much God desires to be near to us in the fact that he doesn't just become present on our altars in the eucharistic liturgy. And he doesn't just dwell within us in Holy Communion. These two facts alone would be amazing enough! But we see his love for us also in the way he remains close to us in the Eucharist, even outside of Mass. Jesus continues to be present in the eucharistic species for as long as the sacred species remain. This is why consecrated eucharistic Hosts are given special reverence inside every Catholic Church. After Mass, the Hosts are placed in a sacred space called a tabernacle that has a candle next to it, reminding us of God's holy presence there.

Now imagine if it were announced that Jesus was going to be at your parish today. Anyone who wanted to meet him and talk to him could stop by and visit with Jesus. What believing Christian would pass up such a wonderful opportunity! Yet, this is what is really happening every day at every Catholic parish where the Eucharist resides in the tabernacle. The same Jesus who walked the streets of Galilee bringing healing, guidance, and strength to those many souls in the first century wants to console, strengthen, and enlighten us today through his abiding presence in the Eucharist.

This is why some Catholics take time occasionally to stop by their churches to make a short "visit" to Jesus in the Blessed Sacrament. They enter their parish church and kneel down in a pew; looking upon the tabernacle, they talk to Jesus as a friend. They tell Jesus they love him. They thank him for his blessings. They ask his forgiveness. They seek his guidance in big decisions and his comfort in their sorrows. They pour out their hearts to him in times of need and beg for his help. As the twentieth-century saint Jose Maria Escriva said, the Eucharist "is God waiting for us, God who loves man, who searches us out, who loves us just as we are—limited, selfish, inconstant, but capable of discovering his infinite affection and of giving ourselves fully to him."[8]

---

[8] St. Jose Maria Escriva, *Christ Is Passing By* (New York: Scepter 1974), 344.

We, of course, can talk to Jesus anywhere and at any time. But in the Eucharist we are drawn to his Real Presence among us in the tabernacles throughout the world. Saint John Paul II reminds us that "Jesus awaits us in this sacrament of love. Let us not refuse the time to go meet him in adoration, in contemplation full of faith.... Let our adoration never cease."[9]

---

[9] *CCC* 1380, quoting John Paul II, *Dominicae Cenae*, February 24, 1980, no. 3.

Chapter Twelve

A Walk through the Mass

Many people's experience of Mass is similar to my Italian cousin Stefano's first experience of an NFL football game. Stefano loves football, but his football is what we in the United States call soccer. American NFL football was completely new to him. So when my family brought him to Soldier's Field in downtown Chicago to watch a Bears game, he was completely lost.

When the Bears sacked the opponent's quarterback, everyone stood up to cheer. Stefano did the same. He screamed, "Yeah!" and then he asked me, "Did the Bears score a point?"

When the referee made a bad call against the Bears, we all stood up and booed. Once again, Stefano did the same, raising his fist in the air and shouting, "Booooo!" And then he asked me, "Did the other team score?"

Finally, when the Bears blocked a punt and returned it for a touchdown, everyone in the stadium was jumping up and down, cheering and give each other "high fives". Stefano did the same, and high-fived the people around him. This time, however, he didn't bother asking me any questions. Amid the pandemonium around us, he just looked at me with a little smile that seemed to say, "I have no idea what's going on ... but I'm sure it's good for the Bears!"

Basilica of Santa Pudenziana, Rome

I think that's how many of us experience the Mass. We stand up, sit down, and kneel with everyone else. We say the responses—"And with your spirit", "Alleluia", "Thanks be to God"—with everyone else. We make the sign of the cross, exchange a sign of peace, and walk up to receive Communion. Like my cousin Stefano at the football game, we sometimes go through all the motions, but we're not sure what it all means.

But if we're attentive to God's Word, we will begin to notice how the prayers, signs, and rituals of the Mass come from Scripture. Whether it be standing and kneeling, or using candles and incense, or praying "The Lord be with you", "Glory to God in the Highest", "Holy, holy, holy, Lord", and "Thanks be to God", practically everything we say and do in the liturgy is rooted in the Bible. The more we understand the significance of these rituals and responses, the more we will experience the Mass as a whole as a beautiful

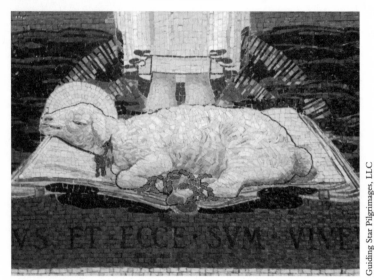

Guiding Star Pilgrimages, LLC

Church of the Transfiguration, detail, Mount Tabor, Israel

prayer in which the God who is love, step-by-step through-out the liturgy, is inviting us to a deeper union with him.[1]

The Two Tables at Mass

The basic structure of the Mass goes all the way back to the early Church, with some of the actual prayers themselves already being recited within just a few generations after the apostles.

The two main parts are the Liturgy of the Word and the Liturgy of the Eucharist. We are fed first at what is sometimes

---

[1] For a fuller explanation of all the prayers and rituals of the Mass, especially in light of their biblical roots, see Edward Sri, *A Biblical Walk through the Mass: Understanding What We Say and Do in the Liturgy* (West Chester, Penn.: Ascension Press, 2011).

called the "table of the Word", where God's inspired Scriptures are proclaimed. Then we are nourished at the "table of the Eucharist", where we receive Christ's Body and Blood in Holy Communion. These two main pillars of the Mass are flanked by smaller sections known as the Introductory Rites and the Concluding Rites. Let's now consider these four sections of the liturgy.

The Introductory Rites

The opening prayers of the Mass are all about preparation. We can't just walk into Mass, go through the motions, and expect the liturgy to bear much fruit in our lives. We need to get ready. We need to transition into this sacred moment and prepare our hearts so that we more fully enter into the Mass. In the Bible, when the ancient Israelites prepared to hear God proclaim the Ten Commandments at Mount Sinai, they consecrated themselves for three days. Similarly, since we at Mass are about to meet God in his inspired Scriptures and in the Eucharist, we also need to get ready.

That's why the very first thing we do is invoke God's presence by making the sign of the cross. This ancient practice of tracing the sign of the cross over our bodies and praying, "In the name of the Father, and of the Son, and of the Holy Spirit", invites God to come into our lives. By starting Mass in this way, we are setting apart this time for God and calling on his holy presence.

Next, the priest says, "The Lord be with you." This is no ordinary greeting, like "Good morning." In the Bible, this expression is used to address people whom God is calling to an important mission—one they could never dare to pursue on their own. They need God's help, and that's why God or an angel says to the person, "The Lord is with you." When we hear those words at Mass, we are being reminded of the daunting, sacred mission God gives to us in the liturgy. What is that mission? We are about to encounter God's Word and God's presence in the Eucharist—not something we should take lightly. We sinners are not worthy to encounter God in this intimate way. But God invites us, and he will help us as we prepare our souls to enter into these sacred mysteries. So when the priest says, "The Lord is with you", it's as if he is saying to us, "Get ready! May God be with you as you prepare for this most sacred encounter."

One of the most important steps in this preparation is to confess our sins and beg for God's forgiveness. That's why we pray, "I confess to Almighty God and to you my brothers and sisters ...", and then we entrust ourselves to his loving mercy, praying, "Lord have mercy.... Christ have mercy.... Lord have mercy." Then, confident in God's steadfast love and mercy, we give praise to God for the forgiveness of sins brought about by Christ as we pray, "Glory to God in the highest!"

Notice how all these introductory prayers and rituals have their purpose. They all fit together. Moving from invoking God's presence in the sign of the cross, to seeking his forgiveness in the "I confess ..." and "Lord have mercy ..." prayers, to thanking him for his salvation in the Gloria, the Introductory Rites help us be ready to encounter God in his Word and in the Eucharist.

Liturgy of the Word

Think of the Liturgy of the Word as a loving dialogue between you and God. Here, God speaks to each of us personally through the inspired words of Scripture. These readings at Mass are not merely stories from a long time ago. Nor

Guiding Star Pilgrimages, LLC

Mass in Shepherd's Fields, outside Bethlehem

do they simply offer moral teachings and spiritual lessons. For the Bible doesn't just speak *about* God. It is *God's own words* in the words of men. And since they are God's words, they transcend time and space and can speak to us today. The same Holy Spirit who inspired the words of Scripture thousands of years ago is alive in our hearts today, prompting us and guiding us to apply it to our lives. It is, therefore, a personal Word spoken anew to the hearts of each individual person at Mass. That's why three people may hear the same reading but each be touched by God in a different way. One might hear something that sheds light on a challenge he is facing in his family, while another person might be inspired to grow in a certain virtue, and still another may find comfort in a time of suffering. As Vatican II taught, "In the sacred books the Father who is in heaven comes lovingly to meet his children, and talks with them."[2]

[2] Vatican II, Dogmatic Constitution on Divine Revelation, *Dei Verbum*, November 18, 1965, no. 21.

The Liturgy of the Word consists of a reading from the Old Testament, followed by a Responsorial Psalm, in which we respond to God's Word, not with our own human words, but with the words of praise and thanksgiving he inspired in the book of Psalms. This is followed by a reading from a New Testament letter, or the Acts of the Apostles, or the book of Revelation. The Liturgy of the Word reaches its climax in the Gospel reading. All the other readings point in some way to Jesus Christ, but the Gospels present the life of Jesus himself. That's why we give special reverence to the Gospel reading: we stand; sing, "Alleluia" (meaning "Praise the Lord!"); have a procession with the book of the Gospels; and trace the sign of the cross over our foreheads, lips, and heart, consecrating all our thoughts, words, and actions to Christ.

Just as the ancient Jews had a three-year cycle of readings in the synagogue, so we have a three-year cycle of readings that present the wide breadth of Sacred Scripture. By simply going to Mass each Sunday, Catholics journey over and over again through the story of biblical salvation history.

After hearing God's Word, the priest or deacon explains the readings and helps us apply them to our lives in the homily. And then we respond to God's Word by renewing our profession of faith in the Creed and by humbly presenting our needs to God in the prayer of the faithful.

The Liturgy of the Eucharist

Now we come to the high point of the Mass. This is the moment when we encounter the God who is love in the most profound way as the priest carries out Jesus' command at the Last Supper. The bread and wine are changed into the Body and Blood of Christ. We are drawn into Christ's sacrificial offering of himself to the Father. And we receive our Lord Jesus in the most intimate Holy Communion.

But this section begins with the Presentation of the Gifts. In the early Church, people brought to Mass the work of their hands—bread, wine, honey, wool, wax, flowers, and other gifts—which represented hours and hours of their lives. These gifts ultimately expressed a gift of themselves to God. Today, a representative of the congregation processes just with gifts of bread and wine and our financial donations to the altar. But these small gifts symbolize the giving of our entire lives to God. This bread and wine is about to be changed into the Body and Blood of Jesus Christ. So don't think of this part of the Mass as "halftime"—a time to check out for a bit. When the people process to the altar with the bread and wine, we should be talking to God in our hearts, uniting all our works, joys, sufferings—our entire lives—with Christ's offering of himself to the Father, which is about to be made sacramentally present.

Next comes the Eucharistic Prayer. The priest begins by exhorting us, "Lift up your hearts." In the Bible, the heart is the center of all our thoughts, desires, and attentions. For the priest to say, "Lift up your hearts," is a summons to give God our best attention right now, to lift up all our thoughts and desires to God, for we are approaching the supreme mysteries of the Mass. Then we sing, "Holy, Holy, Holy, Lord ..."— words that echo what the angels say before God's presence in heaven (see Is 6:3; Rev 4:8). How fitting it is that we do this, for we, like the angels, are about to encounter the all-holy, divine Lord, who will become present on the altar. That happens in the Eucharistic Prayer, in which the priest prays for the Holy Spirit to come down upon the gifts of bread and wine "that they may become the Body and Blood

Basilica of St. John Lateran, main altar, Rome

of our Lord, Jesus Christ", and then he repeats over the bread and wine the words of Jesus at the Last Supper ("This is my body.... This is my blood").

The Liturgy of the Eucharist culminates with what is called the Communion Rite. In just a few moments we will receive Jesus in the Eucharist. Our final preparations involve expressing the unity we have with God and with each other—a twofold unity that will be deepened when we receive Communion. We first recite the Lord's Prayer, in which we express the intimate union we have with God. We recognize our God not just as Creator and Lord, but we affectionately address him as "our Father". And then we express the harmony God desires us to have with each other in the Rite of Peace, which can include some sign (such as shaking hands) that expresses the unity between God's people, which will be deepened in Holy Communion.

Finally, we humbly acknowledge our unworthiness to receive Christ into our souls. We repeat the words of the Roman centurion in the Gospels who wanted Jesus to heal his dying servant, but didn't feel worthy to have Jesus come to his home to perform the healing. The centurion acknowledged his own sinfulness, saying, "Lord, I am not worthy that you should enter under my roof ..."[3] We are like the centurion when we approach Holy Communion at Mass. We know we're not worthy to have Jesus come under the "roof" of our souls, but we entrust ourselves to Christ's mercy, believing that just as he healed the centurion's servant some two thousand years ago, he can heal us as he comes to dwell within us in the Eucharist today.

Concluding Rites: Why the Mass Is Called the "Mass"

The only time the word "Mass" is used in the sacred liturgy is in the conclusion. The priest or deacon says, "Go forth, the Mass is ended." What does the word "Mass" mean? The term is derived from the Latin word *missa*, which means "dismissal" or "sending". It was customary in the ancient world to conclude an assembly with a formal dismissal, and the early Christians did the same, with the priest ending the liturgy with the words *Ite missa est*—meaning, "Go, you are dismissed or sent forth."

It's fascinating that the Church eventually named the entire liturgy after the key word in this concluding line: *missa*. It underscores how the liturgy is actually a going forth,

---

[3] Matthew 8:8 reads, "Lord, I am not worthy to have you come under my roof; but only say the word, and my servant will be healed." Cf. Luke 7:6–7.

a sending. It involves sending us out to bring Christ's love into the world. The closing prayer, therefore, is not a directionless dismissal. It sends us on a crucial mission. As the *Catechism* puts it, "The liturgy in which the mystery of salvation is accomplished concludes with the sending forth (*missio*) of the faithful, so that they may fulfill God's will in their daily lives" (*CCC* 1332). Having encountered God's love in the Eucharist, we are now sent to carry that love out into the world.

Chapter Thirteen

Confession

To the right of the main altar of St. Peter's Basilica in Rome, people from all over the world come to confess their sins to a priest in the sacrament of penance. In this area, there's an interesting mosaic that depicts the biblical account of Jesus rescuing the apostle Peter from sinking in the Sea of Galilee. I like to consider how this beautiful image, standing amid the many confessions taking place here each day, can be seen as making an important point about the sacrament.

In the Gospel account of this scene, Peter had been on a boat with the other apostles one night, when he suddenly saw Jesus walking on the water (see Mt 14:28–33). Peter wanted to join him, so he leapt out of the boat toward Jesus and miraculously started walking on water himself. But when Peter was distracted by the winds and became afraid, he took his eyes off of Christ and began to sink. The mosaic depicts Peter right at that moment, falling in the water and desperately reaching out to Jesus, saying, "Lord, save me!"

The image reminds us that when we, like Peter, take our eyes off of Christ—when we sin—our lives start to sink. But Jesus waits for us in the sacrament of penance. He wants to lift us out of whatever sins, weaknesses, or guilt weigh us down. He wants to forgive us, heal us, and strengthen us so we can walk with him anew. There are many times in our

Jesus walking on Water, Altar of the Navicella,
St. Peter's Basilica, Vatican City

lives when we, like Peter on the Sea of Galilee that night, need to reach out to Jesus in the sacrament and say, "Lord, save me!" Then we can experience the power of Christ lifting us out of our darkness, sins, and whatever is weighing us down in life and experience the dawn of a new day in our relationship with God.

The Truth That Sets You Free

One of the most intriguing aspects of Catholic life is the practice of confession. The whole idea of people unveiling their souls in the confessional, telling the priest their deepest confidences—their sins, weaknesses, ways of hurting others, and failures in their relationship with God—is utterly fascinating to many in our secular world.

But for many faithful Catholics, confession is one of the most powerful, liberating, peace-giving facets of their faith. Confession is one of the few "no spin zones" we have in life, a setting that invites us to be completely vulnerable—honest before God, before the priest, and even before one's self. We don't have many places in life where we can be so in touch with reality.

When we make a good confession, we begin to see ourselves as we really are. We begin to notice the ways pride, envy, or selfishness taint our hearts. We see how we are sometimes motivated by fear, insecurity, profit, or pleasure. We become more aware of the ways our words or actions hurt other people. We also start to recognize the ways we fail to give the best of ourselves to God and to the people in our lives.

Confession invites us to face the truth about ourselves—an important first step in spiritual growth. People who muddle through life rationalizing their sins and never earnestly striving to live more for God and others fail to mature spiritually. It's only when we come "naked" before the Lord—humbled, honest, and sorrowful—that we come to know experientially, in the core of our being, just how dependent we really are on God. Such souls know how little they can do on their own. They want to love more, serve more, and give more. They want to be better husbands and wives, fathers and mothers, friends, colleagues, neighbors, and Christians, but they know they need God's help. It is in such humble souls that God does his greatest work. As the nineteenth-century Catholic writer G. K. Chesterton once quipped, "There are saints indeed in my religion: but a saint only means a man who really knows he is a sinner."[1] In other words, the main

---

[1] G. K. Chesterton, *Alarms and Discussions* (New York: Dodd, Mead, and Company, 1911), 281.

division in the world isn't between sinners and nonsinners. "[A]ll have sinned and fall short of the glory of God" (Rom 3:23). The key difference between those who are on the road to sanctity and those who are not is that some people know quite acutely that they are sinners, while others don't come to terms with the truth about themselves. The regular practice of confession keeps us on the path of holiness by keeping us grounded in the reality of our weak human condition.

But in confession, we also come to know a second truth: the truth of God's steadfast love for us, even with all our weaknesses and sins. God certainly summons us to repent and turn away from sin. But he is patient and merciful with us. He forgives us over and over again and even gives us the grace to help us overcome our sins in the future.

We should not, however, view God's mercy in confession like that of a powerful ruler merely pardoning a wrongdoer in his kingdom. Confession is not a legal process in which we are like spiritual criminals begging the divine Judge to overlook our sins and grant us a pardon. Rather, when we come before God in confession standing on the truth—acknowledging our sins—and we are sincerely sorry for how we lived and desire to change, our heavenly Father sees more than the legal facts of our sins. He sees our hearts. When God sees the positive transformation already taking place in our souls, he rejoices in that. He doesn't just pardon us. He embraces us in love, seeming to forget whatever evil we had committed.[2]

Why Confess to a Priest?

But we must admit that this sacrament might seem a little intimidating to those who have not been to confession in

[2] See John Paul II, *Dives et Misericordia*, November 30, 1980, no. 6.

Door of the Sacraments, St. Peter's Basilica, Vatican City

many years, or to those who have never gone before. And to others in our world, the whole practice of confession seems absurd or even scandalous. "Why do I need to confess my sins to a priest? He can't forgive my sins. He's not God!"

This is a fair question. In the end, we shouldn't put our trust in any human being to forgive our sins, whether that person be a holy, virtuous lay person, priest, or bishop, or even the pope. The Bible, after all, says only God can forgive sins (see Mk 2:7).

So it's true that we should not put all our trust in any human being to forgive our sins. But we should put all our trust in Jesus Christ. And when we look closely at the Scriptures, we can at least begin to see that Jesus wants us to go to the priest to experience the forgiveness that only God can offer us.

The Priest behind the Priest

Only God can forgive sins. And since Jesus is the divine Son of God, he can say that he has "authority on earth to forgive sins". But what's most amazing is that Jesus not only exercised that authority, telling people, "Your sins are forgiven."[3] He also *shared* that mission with his apostles. Jesus gave the apostles a share in his authority to do what he had been doing in his public ministry, a ministry that included preaching the gospel, healing every disease and infirmity, and even forgiving sins (see Mt 10:1–8). This is, in part, why the crowds, after watching Jesus forgive a man's sins, marveled over how God "had given such authority to *men*" (Mt 9:8; emphasis added). Notice how the word here is in the plural: "men". The crowds didn't praise God for giving such authority to one man, Jesus alone, but to men, probably referring to the authority he gave to the apostles who share in his ministry of reconciliation.

That Jesus gave this kind of authority to the apostles becomes explicit after his death and Resurrection. Consider the following account of Jesus' appearance to the disciples on that first Easter Sunday: "'Peace be with you. As the Father has sent me, even so I send you.' And when he had said this, he breathed on them, and said to them, 'Receive the Holy Spirit. If you forgive the sins of any, they are forgiven; if you retain the sins of any, they are retained'" (Jn 20:21–23).

Three points need to be unpacked here. First, Jesus said, "As the Father has sent me, even so I send you." Why did the Father send the Son? To bring forgiveness of sins and reconcile us with God. So when Jesus says, "As the Father has sent

[3] Mt 9:2; Mk 2:5, 10; Lk 7:48.

me, even so I send you," he is commissioning the apostles to participate in his ministry of reconciliation.

Jesus next does something utterly amazing. He breathes the Holy Spirit on them. Here, Jesus bestows on them the power of the Spirit that has been working in him. The same Spirit of Christ that healed the sick, raised people from the dead, and forgave sins throughout his public ministry is given to the apostles. They will now have the power to forgive sins—not on their own authority, but through the Holy Spirit working through them.

Third, Jesus explicitly tells them they have the power to forgive people's sins. He says, "If you forgive the sins of any, they are forgiven." Indeed, Saint Paul the apostle speaks about being entrusted with this kind of "ministry of reconciliation". He doesn't forgive any sin on his own, but he and the apostles represent Christ. They are "ambassadors for Christ" proclaiming "the message of reconciliation": "[B]e reconciled to God" (2 Cor 5:18–20).

Jesus also gave the apostles the authority to reconcile sinners with the Church. He tells the apostles, "[W]hatever you bind on earth shall be bound in heaven, and whatever you loose on earth shall be loosed in heaven" (Mt 18:18). In rabbinic Judaism, the expression "binding and loosing" described a rabbi's teaching and juridical authority, including the authority to ban sinners from the community and restore them as members of the fellowship. Moreover, the Bible itself in several places uses the verb "to loose" to mean "to forgive".[4] Therefore, Jesus' giving the apostles the power to "bind and loose" means he is giving them the authority to forgive sinners and reconcile them with the Church. All these shades to "binding and loosing" apply to

[4] For example, see Job 42:9 LXX; Sir 28:2; Rev 1:5.

Guiding Star Pilgrimages, LLC

St. Peter, Church of St. Peter in Gallicantu, Jerusalem

the way Jesus entrusted his apostles with teaching, administering Church discipline, and absolving or retaining sins in his name.[5]

Can't I Go to God Directly?

None of this should be surprising. Throughout the Bible, God has always used human beings as his instruments to carry out his plan of salvation.[6] God worked through Moses to part the waters of the Red Sea. He worked through the prophet Elijah to raise a child from the dead. And he worked through

---

[5] For more on the sacrament of penance and Scripture, see Scott Hahn, *Lord Have Mercy* (New York: Image, 2003).

[6] See Ex 14:21; 1 Kings 17:20–20; 2 Kings 5:1–44.

the prophet Elisha to cure a man of leprosy. If God regularly appointed leaders to carry out his miracles in the Old Testament, it shouldn't surprise us that he continues to invite men and women to participate in his works of salvation today— saving works that include forgiving sins.

Those coworkers of Christ today are the bishops and priests who, through their ordination, continue the mission Jesus entrusted to the apostles until the end of time. They are Christ's "ambassadors". Jesus works through them, forgiving sins, "binding and loosing", and carrying out the "ministry of reconciliation". In the sacrament of penance, our sins are forgiven, not by the priest's own power, but by Jesus working through the priest. That's why when we go to confession, we should always see the Priest behind the priest: Jesus Christ.

Some still may wonder, "But why can't I go to God directly?" As Catholics, we should go to God every day on our own, asking him to forgive our sins. The practice of making a daily "examination of conscience" is important. Many saints and spiritual leaders encourage us to take a few moments near the end of each day to examine our consciences, which simply means that we prayerfully consider the ways we failed to love God and neighbor that day, and then tell God we're sorry and ask his forgiveness. We don't need a priest or a sacrament to do this. Christians should do this every night on their own.

But this is not enough. We also need to frequent the sacrament of penance. In reality, the most direct and powerful way to experience Christ's forgiveness is to go to his appointed ambassadors—the priests—and encounter Jesus in the sacrament of reconciliation. God's mercy certainly is not limited to the sacrament, but confession is the ordinary means through which Christ intends to forgive us. And going to the sacrament comes with many benefits.

First, souls that approach the sacrament with sincere and contrite hearts usually experience a great peace of conscience when their sins are forgiven. This makes sense, even in ordinary individual relationships. When, for example, I've done something to cause tension or misunderstanding with a friend, family member, or spouse, a lack of peace abides in the relationship. That disharmony will continue to fester in the relationship in subtle ways until I recognize deep in my heart the wrong I have done and am sorrowful over it. But even this recognition is not enough to mend a relationship. Only when I actually tell the other person "I am sorry" and the other person forgives me is peace truly restored and the relationship can move on, grow, and deepen. Some of the most profound moments of growth in my marriage, for example, have come when I've spoken to my wife those three crucial words—"I am sorry"—and have heard her reply, "I forgive you." How freeing those words are!

Similarly, in our relationship with God, our sins need to be brought out into the light. We have a need to speak our sins and express our sorrow. We also have a need to *hear* that we are forgiven. That's how God made us. And that's why God gave us the sacrament of penance. In confession, we speak our sins. We say them aloud to God in the presence of his representative minister, the priest. And we then need to hear from the priest that our sins are indeed forgiven: "I absolve you of all your sins." How liberating it is to go through this process! How freeing it is to hear God, through the priest, tell us that our sins are forgiven. People who regularly go to confession often describe how this sacrament is one of the greatest blessings of being Catholic and is a profound moment of spiritual growth.

A second blessing of the sacrament of penance is that it reconciles us with the Church. Since all our sins are never

Basilica of St. John Lateran, detail, Rome

From the *Symbolon* series

completely private ones—they all in some way effect our relationship with the body of Christ—we must be reconciled, not just with God, but the Church. It is fitting, therefore, that we confess our sins to a representative of the Church, the priest.

Third, the sacrament strengthens us, giving us the grace to overcome our sins in the future. If we want to grow in the spiritual life—if we want to tap into Christ's power to heal our weaknesses, to conquer bad habits, and to avoid falling into the same temptations in the future—we should go to the sacrament of penance often. In the sacrament, we are not only forgiven of our sins; we also receive "an increase of spiritual strength for the Christian battle" (*CCC* 1496).

Catholic Sanity

There is one lesson I will never forget from my introductory sociology class in college: "Catholics are some of the most

sane people in the world." That's what my Jewish professor said, and I was shocked. (I knew a lot of Catholics and
thought some were pretty crazy!) The professor explained
that with the ritual of confession, practicing Catholics had a
regular outlet for facing the wrong they have done, dealing
with guilt, and starting over in life.

I don't recall if his claim was based on a sociological study
or just his own opinion, but the insight certainly points to
something true. God made us, and he knows how we work.
He knows we have a need to face the truth about our lives,
to get things off our chests, and to be forgiven and start anew.
That's why he gave us the sacrament of reconciliation.

Sadly, many people go through their whole lives never
coming to terms with their sins and weaknesses. They never
take responsibility for their actions. They rationalize their
selfish decisions and their neglect of family and friends. They
always make excuses for their own shortcomings, while
blaming others for the problems in their lives. Such people
are not living in reality. To keep up the illusion they have of
themselves, they desperately cling to a thousand defense
mechanisms and dysfunctions that help them avoid facing the
truth about their lives.

But Jesus wants to free us from all that. He wants to liberate us from our bad habits, sins, and self-deception. When
we come before God in the sacrament of reconciliation, we
have a regular opportunity to face the truth about our lives.
God knows it's good for us to recognize our faults. And God
knows we need to experience his forgiveness and trust in his
grace to help us live more like Christ. That's why God gave
us the sacrament of penance. And that's why we should go to
confession often throughout the year. Many spiritual advisors
recommend going about once a month. Saintly Christians,
such as John Paul II, went every day.

"Lord, Save Me!"

The sacrament of reconciliation is a beautiful encounter with Christ's mercy—one that takes a weight off our shoulders, keeps us from drowning in our sinful habits, and gives us a chance to start anew. But we should ask ourselves what might be keeping us from encountering Christ in confession more often. Are we too busy, making other things in our lives more important? Are we too nervous to speak of our sins in the person of the priest? Or are we just afraid to change and don't want to admit our faults?

Remember, no matter what you have done and no matter how long you have been away from confession, Jesus wants to forgive you. He is waiting for you in the sacrament. So if you ever feel your life is offtrack and that you are starting to sink, all you have to do is reach out to Jesus in confession. Just like Peter cried out to the Lord and was saved on the Sea of Galilee, you can cry out to Jesus in the sacrament of penance and say, "Lord, save me"—confident that Christ's merciful hand is already there reaching out to you.

Chapter Fourteen

A Catholic Moral Worldview

How does one talk about morality in a world that no longer believes in moral truth?

The pervasive mindset today is that of moral relativism—the idea that there are no moral standards for anyone. Each individual decides for *himself* what is right or wrong. A relativist says you can have "your truth" and I can have "my truth", but there is no "real truth" to which we are all accountable. In such a culture, morality seems to be just a bunch of rules—arbitrary rules set up by one group of people imposing their views on others.

But what if God placed on man's heart a desire for beatitude—for true, lasting happiness? And what if that happiness is found in living a certain kind of life, in love with God and the people God has placed in our lives? And what if God loves us so much he actually showed us what that good life looks like and revealed to us the pathway to happiness?

This is what Catholic morality is really all about: the quest for happiness. Many today have the impression that Christianity is centered on rules for behavior, submitting to God's random decrees so you don't get punished. Catholic morality, however, emphasizes that God loves us, has a plan for our lives, and wants us to be happy. And he gave us a moral roadmap, not as arbitrary rules to follow, but as a guide to our flourishing. As such, Catholic morality is much more about

From the Symbolon series

Temperance (detail in Cardinal and Theological Virtues by Raphael), Vatican Museums, Vatican City

helping me becoming the kind of person God made me to be, so that I can find fulfillment in life.

That's why having a Catholic moral worldview is absolutely critical, not just to be a good Catholic, but to live a fully human life. So if your heart longs for something more than the mediocre, "anything goes" culture around you—if you desire to make your life something beautiful, something noble, something even heroic—then step back with me now, as we consider some of the key features of that moral vision that corresponds to your heart's deepest desires.

The Pathway to Happiness

One key aspect of a Catholic moral worldview is a proper understanding of God's moral law. Why does God give a moral law? Why does any good, loving father give a moral law?

As a dad, I sometimes have to give rules to my children. "Don't touch the stove.... Don't play in the street.... Don't play with matches." I give them these rules, not because I want to control them or keep them from having fun, but because I love my kids, want what's best for them, and want them to be happy. I don't want them to get hurt. The rules are an expression of my love for them. The law flows from my fatherly heart.

Similarly, God loves us and wants us to be happy. That's why he revealed himself to us and gave us his law. In his Son, Jesus Christ, God shows us most fully the kind of life that will make us happy—a life of total, self-giving love. And through the Bible and the Church, God gives us certain moral laws to keep us on this path to happiness. Far from restricting us, God's moral law gives us the freedom to live life well.

God's moral law is like an instruction manual for our lives. The instruction manual for my computer, for example, warns me not to put it in water. The manufacturers know that water can damage my computer, so they give me that warning because they want the computer to function well for me.

But imagine if I interpreted their warning as something oppressive. Imagine if upon reading the instruction manual, I felt that the manufacturer was trying to control me, not help me. Imagine if I angrily ripped up the instruction manual, called the computer company on the phone, and yelled at them, saying, "This is *my* computer now. I am free to do whatever I want with my computer. Who are you to tell me what to do with my computer? Stop imposing your views about computers on me!"

Can I disregard the manufacturer's warning and take my computer with me when I jump into the swimming pool?

Absolutely. But I'll destroy the computer when I do! Similarly, am I able to disregard God's moral law and just live however I please as if his law has no relevance for my life? Sure. But I'll do damage to myself, hurt others in the process, and never find the true happiness for which I long. This is why sin is *not* about breaking some random religious rule. It's about failing to live according to the greatness for which God made us.

Think of God's moral law—whether found in the Ten Commandments, the Bible, or the teachings of Christ and the Church—as the instruction manual for our happiness. It's given for our good. God is the divine manufacturer. He made us, and he knows how we work. He knows that if we do certain things, we will be happy. And he knows that if we do other things, we won't function well. We will hurt others, hurt ourselves, and fail to experience the happiness he wants for us. Far from inhibiting, the moral law is actually liberating. It shows us the way to a fully human life, which is the only way we will find our happiness. As the psalmist says to God, "Your word is a lamp to my feet and a light to my path" (Ps 119:105).

Freedom

A second key feature of a Catholic moral worldview is a proper understanding of freedom. For the modern world, freedom is simply the power to choose. It's a "negative" view of freedom in the sense that it only considers being free *from* outside forces controlling me. In this perspective, I possess freedom when I don't have others interfering in my life and I can make choices for myself. There are no good or bad choices. It doesn't matter *what* I choose. All that matters is *that* I choose.

Love Unveiled

Moses, by Michaelangelo. Basilica of St. Peter in Chains, Rome

True freedom, however, is not simply the ability to make choices. It's the ability to perform actions with excellence. And excellence requires certain skills. Take, for example, speaking a foreign language. Are you free to speak Russian? Your government may not interfere with your attempts to speak the language. And your employer, friends, church, and family members may be supportive as well. But in the classical perspective, you would only have the freedom to speak Russian when you've acquired the skill of conversing in this language. Without the basic language skill, you simply are not free to speak Russian, no matter how much you may want to.

Similarly, are you free to play the violin? You may enjoy the instrument and desire to play it. But unless you have acquired the skill of playing violin through lessons, practice, and hard work, you are not free to play this stringed instrument. You may be able to make painful, screeching noises with the violin, but you are not free to play it with excellence. Skills give you the ability to perform certain actions with excellence.

Now here's a more crucial question: Are you free to be a good husband or wife? Are you free to be a good mother or father? Are you free to be a good friend, a good neighbor, a good employee, a good citizen? Living out our relationships with excellence requires a lot more than feelings, desires, and good intentions. As with speaking a language and playing a musical instrument, living our relationships well also requires certain skills. Those basic life skills are called virtues.

Virtue

Here we come to a third key aspect of a Catholic moral worldview: virtue. The *Catechism* defines virtue as the habitual disposition to do the good (see *CCC* 1803). When we possesses a virtue, we are able to act toward the good consistently and promptly, with ease and with joy. Think of the virtues as the life skills we need to live our relationships well. I need virtues such as generosity, humility, patience, courage, and self-control to love my spouse, children, coworkers, and friends. If, for example, I am a generous man, I consistently make sacrifices for others, putting others' needs before my own. When someone needs my time, attention, or resources, it's easy for me to put aside my own interests to help others. It's second nature to me. It's simply part of who I am. Generosity is one of the steady virtues I need to love the people in my life.

When I lack virtue, however, my defect in character doesn't just affect me. It hinders my ability to love the people around me. For example, if I lack in the virtue of generosity, I will do selfish things that hurt my spouse. If I lack prudence and spend too many hours preoccupied with work and not enough energy investing personally in my children, my kids will feel the effects. If I often get overwhelmed with life and become easily irritated, stressed out, or lose my temper, the people in my life will suffer the consequences of my lack of patience. If I spend hours and hours playing video games or watching TV, it's probably not going to be easy for me to make sacrifices to serve others, because I'm constantly entertaining myself.

This is why deficiency in virtue is so tragic—to the extent that I lack virtue, I am not free to love. No matter how much I may desire to be a good son of God, a good husband to my wife, and a good father to my children, without virtue, I will not consistently give the best of myself to the Lord, I will not honor and serve my wife effectively, and I will not raise my children as well as I should. My lack of virtue will affect other people's lives. Here we can begin to see that true freedom is not merely the ability to make choices. It's found in the ability to consistently make *good* choices—virtuous choices—that enable us to live our relationships with excellence.

Made for Friendship

Catholic morality encourages us to grow in virtue so that we can be the best friends, citizens, spouses, parents, and children of God we can be. And this brings us to a fourth key feature of a Catholic moral worldview: we are made for friendship—friendship with God and the people God has placed in our lives. The God who is love created us freely

Guiding Star Pilgrimages, LLC.

Mount of the Beatitudes Church, Israel

out of love and created us *to* love. Indeed, we are made in
the image and likeness of the Holy Trinity, the three divine
Persons who live in communion together in total self-giving
love. We are, therefore, made for relationships, to live like
the Trinity, giving ourselves in love to others.

That's why Jesus summed up the Christian life not *legally*
but *relationally*. When someone asked Jesus which of the
commandments are the greatest, he focused on love of God
and love of neighbor (see Mk 12:30–32). In other words,
morality is not about random religious rules to follow, but
the path to living out our relationships with God and neighbor well. And it's only in living these relationships well that
we will find fulfillment in life.

But the modern individualistic view of freedom hurts
the very relationships we're made for. It gets us to seek our

happiness by turning inward to self instead of looking outward toward others. It encourages us to pursue personal advantage, comfort, and pleasure *more than* to seek what's best for the people in our lives. Instead of encouraging people to grow in virtue and be the best spouses, parents, friends, coworkers, and citizens they can be, the self-centered notion of freedom just says, "Be yourself. Be your own person. Do whatever you want with your life."

This focus on the self even leads us to view other people sometimes as *obstacles* to our personal fulfillment. Joseph Ratzinger (Pope Benedict XVI) put it this way:

> If the autonomous [self] has the last word, then its desires are simply unlimited. It then wants to snatch as much from life as it can get out of it. This is, I think, really a very major problem of life today. People say: Life is basically complicated and short; I want to get as much out of it as possible, and no one has the right to stand in my way. Before all else I have to be able to seize my piece of it, to fulfill myself, and no one has the right to interfere with me. Anyone who would stand in my way is an enemy of my very self.[1]

The Problem of Moral Relativism

This individualistic concept of freedom is at the very heart of moral relativism. If all that matters is that I have the freedom to choose what I want to do in life, then there are no good or bad choices. If I value the freedom to pursue my desires more than anything else, then the very idea of a moral law is a threat to my willfulness. Instead of seeing Christ's moral

---

[1] Joseph Ratzinger, *Salt of the Earth* (San Francisco: Ignatius Press, 1997), 167.

teachings like a roadmap helping me get to where I want to go in life, I view it as something in my way, something oppressive, telling me what to do. "It's *my* life. I can do what I want with it. Don't impose your morality on me!"

A whole array of injustices is covered in the name of "freedom" and moral relativism. If a wealthy person, for example, doesn't want to share his wealth with the poor, relativism says, "That's his personal lifestyle choice and we shouldn't impose our views on him, even if people will suffer for his lack of generosity." If a husband wants to run off with another woman whom he believes will bring him more emotional fulfillment, who's to say that what he is doing is wrong? His personal choice is more important than his commitment to his family, even if his wife and children suffer because of his decision. If parents are too busy pouring their lives into their careers and hobbies and don't spend as much time giving themselves to their children, that's their choice. We as relativists can't say they are doing anything wrong, even if the children feel the effects of their neglect.

Relativism covers up our selfishness. If there is no moral standard outside ourselves, calling us to give more, love more, and serve more—if all that matters is personal choice—then we can justify the way we neglect our parents, disregard the poor and suffering, back out of commitments to our spouse and children, use other people sexually, and fail to care for the weakest members of society, such as the elderly, the handicapped, and the unborn. Remember, in the world of relativism, it doesn't matter *what* you choose to do with your life. All that matters is *that* you choose. So a relativistic culture, in the end, encourages you to do whatever selfishly pleases you—no matter how your choices may impact others.

Mount of Beatitudes, Israel

Called to Greatness

Ironically, however, this modern "I'm free to do whatever I want" attitude leads to slavery. If I am always striving to do whatever I want, when I want, how I want, and as often as I want, I'm not really free. I actually become a slave—a slave to my selfish desires. And when I'm dominated by my own interests, comforts, and pleasures, it's not easy for me to serve others. I'm not free to love the people in my life effectively, because I'm too caught up in myself.

A Catholic moral vision, however, summons us to rise above the self-centered mentality of our age. It calls us to grow in virtue and seek what is best for others. It inspires us to make sacrifices and to pick up the cross, for the sake of God and neighbor. Most of all, it calls us to live according to our dignity as sons and daughters of God, to live like Jesus Christ in total self-giving love.

This is where our true freedom is found. When we give up our freedom to do whatever we want all the time, we discover a greater freedom: the freedom to love. And this is where we will find our true happiness. As Vatican II taught, "Man cannot find himself except through a sincere gift to others."[2] In other words, it's only when we live for others and not for ourselves that we will find our happiness. When we grow in virtue and fulfill our responsibilities to our parents, spouse, children, friends, and coworkers, we discover the fulfillment God intends for us.

Some might think this kind of committed, sacrificial love is somehow stifling or limiting. But giving love is not the same as other transactions in life. If I give away a twenty-dollar bill to you, I no longer have the bill. If I give my computer to you as a gift, I no longer have my computer. But love works differently. When we give of ourselves to the people in our lives, we don't lose anything. Rather, we gain so much more. Our lives are enriched because we're living the way God made us—we are living like God himself, in total self-giving love.

* * * * *

As we've seen throughout this book, we can't live out this call to love on our own. We need Christ's Spirit within us, changing our weak hearts. We need his grace that comes to us through the Church, the sacraments, and a life of prayer. The drama and beauty of the moral life, therefore, can't be separated from the rest of the Catholic faith. At the center of

[2] Vatican II, Pastoral Constitution on the Church in the Modern World, *Gaudium et Spes*, December 7, 1965, no. 24.

Catholic morality is living in union with Christ—our cooperation with grace and with the promptings of the Holy Spirit—so that Christ's love can radiate ever more through us, helping us to love more and more like him.

And when we live out this beautiful moral vision, we live a fuller life, and, as a result, we give glory to God. For as the second-century Saint Ireneaus once said, "The Glory of God is man fully alive."[3]

[3] St. Irenaeus, *Adv. Haeres* 4, 20, 7: *PG* 7/1, 1037.

Chapter Fifteen

Love and Responsibility

Life, Sex, and Care for the Poor

"[A]m I my brother's keeper?" (Gen 4:9). This was Cain's response of indifference when God asked him about his murdered brother. All too often this is the underlying attitude that characterizes our relationships in the modern world. The individualistic mindset prevalent today gets us to shun our responsibility toward others, whether for the poor and suffering in the world or for people right in our own families, friendships, and romantic relationships. Instead of living in solidarity with our brothers and sisters, we act in a way that basically says, "Am I my brother's keeper?"

We see this in many areas of life today, but we will focus just on three: care for the poor, our romantic relationships, and the way we treat human life.

Care for the Poor

Blessed Mother Teresa often spoke about how the gospel can be summed up on five fingers. While pointing to each finger she would repeat these five words of Jesus from the Gospel of Matthew, chapter 25: "You-did-it-to-me." In this passage,

From the *Symbolon* series

Mother Teresa, outside San Gregorio, Rome

Jesus said those who provide for the hungry, welcome the stranger, clothe the naked, and visit the sick perform these charitable acts ultimately for him.

When we give to the poor, we are giving to God, who is especially present in the poor. For Jesus said, "Truly, I say to you, as you did it to one of the least of these my brethren, you did it to me" (Mt 25:40).

But Pope Francis said that many forces in our modern world undermine our solidarity with the poor. The problem is not just that there are many poor and suffering people in the world and we don't do much about it. That alone is quite tragic. But the deeper problem, according to Pope Francis, is that we tend to overlook our self-centered lifestyle and don't even see our neglect of the poor as a problem.

New ideologies, rampant individualism, and materialistic consumerism weaken social bonds and create what he calls a "globalization of indifference". It's as if modern men and women are trained to run after their own "selfish ideal"— their own fun times, pleasure, advantage, or gain—more than they are trained to find fulfillment in seeking what's best for others and pursuing a common good together. So we don't just neglect the needy among us. We become indifferent to them. It's as if they don't exist to us. In a "culture of exclusion" such as our own, we ignore the needs of our brothers and sisters because we're so caught up in our own careers, families, and entertainments. Pope Francis once said, "Almost without being aware of it, we end up being incapable of feeling compassion at the outcry of the poor, weeping for other people's pain, and feeling a need to help them, as though all this were someone else's responsibility and not our own."[1]

We might have a fleeting moment of sympathy for the poor, but do we feel the weight of our responsibility to care for the weakest members of society? Do we actually give of ourselves to those in need? There are two basic things every Christian should do to overcome this individualistic mentality that gets us to neglect our responsibility to the poor: give more generously of our wealth and possessions and give more of ourselves. When we do this, we not only help our suffering brethren; we also grow in love for Christ, who is present in the poor.

A Culture of Encounter

The Christian is called to be a "faithful and wise steward" in Christ's kingdom (Lk 12:42). In Scripture, a steward managed the affairs and finances of a large household on behalf of his master (see Lk 16:1–8). The wealth, possessions, and land are not his own. He just administers the ruler's household in his stead. This biblical understanding reminds us that, as

---

[1] Francis, Apostolic Exhortation *Evangelii Gaudium*, November 24, 2013, no. 54.

stewards in God's kingdom, all we possess is not our own; it has been entrusted to us by the Lord. We are stewards called to faithfully and wisely manage the Lord's gifts, so that they can be put to good service for his household, the kingdom of God.

In this light, charitable giving is not so much about giving up "my" money to help other people. All I have has been given to me by the Lord, and I am called to manage these gifts wisely as his steward. My wealth is not my own to use however I selfishly please. When I give to the poor, therefore, I am simply being a good steward of the Lord's blessings, using them as he desires. In this sense, giving to the poor is not so much an act of charity as it is an act of justice. As Saint Gregory the Great taught, "When we attend to the needs of those in want, we give them what is theirs not ours."[2]

At the same time, this understanding of stewardship challenges us to examine carefully how we use these gifts from God. When we receive a paycheck, do we think only about how we can spend our money for our own plans and dreams, or do we also think about how we can use our resources to help others? Do we think only about how to build up reserves for our own feeling of security, or are we generous in sharing what God has given to us with those who are barely surviving day-to-day? At the end of our lives, we will have to render an account of how we used our wealth and possessions. Whatever latest device I purchased or how much I had in my savings account won't matter when I go before the judgment seat of God, where Jesus looks at all the poor and suffering in the world and says, "[A]s you did it to one of the least of these my brethren [i.e., not sharing your resources with them], you did it to me." Saint John Chrysostom bluntly describes what's

---

[2] St. Gregory the Great, *Regula Pastoralis*, 2, 21: PL 77, 87.

really happening when we pursue much comfort and financial security for ourselves while miserly giving only our leftovers to the poor. He says, "Not to share one's wealth with the poor is to steal from them."[3]

But we're also called to give something much more valuable than money to the poor: we're called to give of ourselves. It's easy to put a check in the mail or hand some coins to a homeless person on the street. But do we take time to encounter the poor, the sick, and the suffering around us? Do we look them in the eye? Do we talk with them? Pope Francis challenges us to encounter the poor as persons.

> I sometimes ask people: "Do you give alms?" They say to me: "Yes, Father". "And when you give alms, do you look the person you are giving them to in the eye?" "Oh, I don't know, I don't really notice". "Then you have not really encountered him. You tossed him the alms and walked off. When you give alms, do you touch the person's hand or do you throw the coin?". "No, I throw the coin". "So you did not touch him. And if you don't touch him you don't meet him".[4]

Pope Francis calls us to build a culture of encounter—a culture in which we go out of ourselves and have a personal connection with others, including those in need. We must truly look at them, listen to them, and treat them as friends—as brothers and sisters. When he was archbishop of Buenos Aires, Pope Francis would go out at night onto the streets looking for the poor. And he didn't just hand out

---

[3] St. John Chrysostom, *De Lazaro Conzio*, II, 6: *PG* 48, 992D.

[4] "Video Message of Holy Father Francis to the Faithful of Buenos Aires on the Occasion of the Feast of Saint Cajetan", August 7, 2013, http://w2.vatican.va/content/francesco/en/messages/pont-messages/2013/documents/papa-francesco_20130807_videomessaggio-san-cayetan.html.

food. He brought a meal and sat down to eat with them and talk with them. He shared life with them. Pope Francis' example calls us to do the same.

Serving the poor will take on a variety of forms for different people, but we are all called to share in this responsibility. And most of us could do more. But this call to serve those in need is not some ideal Christian ethic only for the Mother Teresas of this world. It actually points to a happier way of life for all of us—a life lived more in solidarity with others and in deeper union with Christ. For when we live our lives more in service to those in need, we not only help those people; we also begin to experience a change in our own hearts. According to Pope Benedict, we become conquered by love.[5] Indeed, almsgiving and care for the poor were some of the chief signs of Christian identity in the early Church. A soul who truly encounters Christ's love, who lives deeply in that love day-to-day, will be moved with compassion to love his brethren more generously. Charitable works are thus a sign of the true disciples of Jesus. They are "persons moved by Christ's love, persons whose hearts Christ has conquered with his love, awakening within them a love of neighbor".[6]

Our Romantic Relationships

A second area where the individualistic mentality of our age hurts us in in our romantic relationships.

Why do so many romantic relationships today—whether it be dating or marriage—begin with great enthusiasm but end in such disappointment and disillusionment? Why do

[5] See Benedict XVI, *Deus Caritas Est*, December 25, 2005, no. 33.
[6] Ibid.

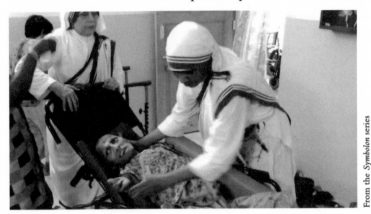

Missionary of Charity Sisters Caring for the Sick, Calcutta, India

From the *Symbolon* series

many people today have the painful experience of being in a relationship they thought was about love, only to realize that the other person was not really committed to them—they were more in it for themselves? Part of the challenge may be our understanding of what love is.

Today, we use the word "love" for many things. We say, "I love chocolate. I love coffee. I love this song. I love my favorite sports team." When we use the word "love" in this way, we simply mean that these things do something for me. They bring me enjoyment, fun, and pleasure. I get something out of them.

But when a husband says to his wife, "I love you," it should mean something more than "You do something for me that I really enjoy" or "I love you because I get something out of you." True love is to will the good of another—to seek what's best for the other person (see *CCC* 1766). It's a commitment to the person for who they are, not to what I get out of the person.

To build a romantic relationship on strong foundations, it's important to understand the difference between two kinds of love: eros and agape.

Eros and Agape

In the valley of the Coliseum in Rome stand the remains of the largest temple of ancient Rome: a temple dedicated to the goddesses Venus and Roma. Venus was the goddess of love and beauty and was associated with one common pagan understanding of love as eros—the passionate love that suddenly comes upon us and seeks pleasure in the beloved.

Eros looks inward and focuses on the good feelings and pleasure one experiences in a romantic relationship. But is there something more? Is there something more to love than just attraction, emotion, and sensual pleasure?

We've seen that true love is about willing the good of the other. It's seeking the good of the other person. That's why the Bible rarely uses the word eros. It instead often uses another Greek word to describe love, the word "agape". In Scripture, agape refers to a total, unconditional, and sacrificial love.

So we should ask ourselves in our relationships, do I tend to focus more on eros, on what feelings I get out of the relationship? Or do I focus more on agape and truly seek what's good for the other person?

Imagine being in a relationship built on agape. The other person is truly committed to you. He wants what's best for *you*. He's not in it for himself. In a relationship built more on eros, however, the other person is not really committed to you. He's more committed to what he gets out of you, whether it be feelings or pleasure or fun times. But what happens when the relationship gets difficult and challenging, when the feelings start to fade and the good times aren't always there? How confident are you that the other person really will stay with you? Like the ruined temple of Venus in Rome, a relationship built on self-seeking love will not stand the test of time.

Love and Sexuality

Emotional and sensual attractions in themselves certainly are not bad. They spark an initial interest that can lead to love for another person. But for true love to develop, these attractions of eros must ascend to the level of agape, so that love becomes more than an inward feeling.[7] It becomes an outward gift of one's self and a pursuit of the good of the other person, not just one's own enjoyment. "However, when *eros* is taken completely separately from *agape*, it becomes selfish, not focused on the other, and can turn into a using of the other person."[8] This is especially true in the sexual sphere.

Many people today treat sex as merely a physical act—just one of many recreational activities that are enjoyable. "Let's watch a movie. Let's eat some ice cream. Let's have sex."

But the Catholic Church sees in our sexuality something so much more beautiful than this. Sex is not just about pleasure, and it's not just a physical act. It's a profoundly *personal* act meant to draw a man and woman into a deeper union, a deeper love. While the old pop song asked, "What's

---

[7]For more on men-women relationships and the interplay between emotional and sensual attraction and authentic self-giving love, see Edward Sri, *Men, Women and the Mystery of Love: Practical Insights from John Paul II's Love and Responsibility* (Cincinnati: Servant Books, 2007).

[8]*Deus Caritas Est*, no. 5.

Mother Teresa's Room, Missionaries of Charity
Mother House, Calcutta, India

love got to do with it?" the Catholic Church would answer, "Everything."

One key to grasping the Catholic vision for sex is to understand how what we do in our bodies expresses our souls, our very selves. My body is not a machine I reside in. It's intrinsic to who I am. I express myself and interact with others through my body. For example, imagine if someone were to hit you on the face and say, "*I* didn't hit you. My *hand* did that." You're probably not going to accept that! Deep down, we all know that whatever we choose to do with our bodies expresses our very selves.

This has important consequences for understanding sexual intercourse. Sex is the most intimate, physical union two people can have. And this profound union is not just about bodies being joined together and pleasure. The physical union is meant to express a personal union. Sex is an expression of total love, total trust, and total commitment. In giving their bodies to each other, couples are giving their very selves to each other.

Do we view sex this way? Do we view sex as a way of deepening personal union and expressing total commitment to our beloved? Is sex for us an expression of agape (unconditional, committed love)? Or do we approach sex more as a physical act with someone who happens to give us pleasure?

Total Gift of Self

Treating sex as a total gift of one's self corresponds to our heart's deepest desires. We long for a love that lasts, a relationship in which we can give ourselves completely to another person and be accepted by that person as a gift. But we can do things with our sexuality that hinder love and prevent love from maturing. *Lustful thoughts* and *pornography*, for example, train us to view the opposite sex not as persons with dignity—not as persons worthy of love and respect—but as mere objects to exploit in our imagination for our own sensual pleasure. The *casual sex* of the hookup culture treats sex as a recreational sport and has more in common with animal sexuality, which is based on instinct and is completely impersonal, than it does with a human act of love. For many today, sex is just about someone satisfying a need like a hungry dog, a thirsty rabbit, or a cat in heat.

The Catholic vision of sex, however, is so much greater than this. It aims to draw out our deepest desires, which are for love—a love that flows ultimately from the heart, not from the sexual urge. Sex is a profound expression of that longing for communion with our beloved, for total self-giving and acceptance, for what Saint John Paul II called "ecstasy", which means "going out of one's self".[9] But to make this kind of total gift of one's self to another—and to be fully accepted by your beloved as a gift—requires commitment ("I am truly committed to you"). It requires permanence ("This is a lasting love; I am committed to you for the rest of my life"). And it requires a certain exclusivity ("This is something only you and I share"). This, of course, is the unique, committed, faithful love found only in marriage. In marriage, I can completely entrust myself—my emotional center—into the care of my beloved, and I welcome my beloved as a most valuable gift for which I must take great care. Sex in *this* context becomes true ecstasy—an expression of my going out of myself, to give myself as I really am, totally, to my beloved.

A hookup or open-ended relationship cannot provide the secure arena for self-giving and for being received as a valuable gift. That's why sex outside of marriage always involves some kind of use, in which couples treat each other like objects to be used for pleasure, for the feeling of closeness, for the security of having a boyfriend or girlfriend, or for avoiding the fear of being alone.

Sex outside of marriage can create an impression of a closeness that does not really exist between two people. In their bodies they say, "I'm totally yours." But in reality, their hearts merely say, "I'm yours ... until someone better comes along." In such a relationship, the other person is not truly committed to you as a person. They are more committed to the sensual pleasure and emotions they derive from you. And

---

[9] Karol Wojtyla, *Love and Responsibility* (San Francisco: Ignatius Press, 1981), p. 126.

they could just as easily get their sexual and emotional needs met from someone else down the road.

As such, the lack of committed love breeds fear and insecurity in a sexual relationship. Deep down, you know you can't let the other person see you as you really are. You have to act a certain way, dress a certain way, avoid certain topics, and do all you can to keep the other person happy and pleased with you—for you fear that if the relationship gets difficult, challenging, or unpleasant in any way, your beloved will leave you to find someone else. It's like constantly being on a job interview, always needing to impress, and never fully letting your guard down. But is this the kind of love you want? Think about this: No matter how much sex you may have together, without the total commitment of marriage, how much can you really hope to experience the total love you long for? How much can you realistically hope to entrust yourself, as you truly are, to your beloved and be treated by him as a gift of tremendous value? The *Catholic* view of sex as being for marriage is *not* about suppressing desire. It's about protecting relationships so that we might have our deepest desires—the longings in our hearts for authentic agape love—fulfilled.

Human Life: The Powerful against the Weak

The modern individualistic outlook also gets us to shun our responsibility for the weakest members of society, those who need our care and attention the most. People who live comfortable lives—people with health, wealth, and power—are tempted to put their own interests before serving the needs of those who are sick, handicapped, elderly, or dying. We might even view the weak not as persons but as obstacles getting in the way of our self-centered pursuits. Taking time to visit and care for my elderly parents, for example, is considered burdensome, getting in the way of my career, my vacation plans, and my free time with friends and family. Similarly, many individuals who could not handle having a child with a severe illness or disability have walked away from their marriage and family to search for an easier life for themselves. In some circles, the handicapped, sick, and dying are looked at primarily as a financial burden to the family and to taxpayers' dollars. Some might even suggest it's better to get rid of them than have to take care of them.

People who are weak and suffering demand more out of me. They call me to love more, to give more, and to sacrifice more. But such self-giving is too much for me. My interests are more important than my responsibilities to these people who need my love. As Saint John Paul II once said, "A life which would require greater acceptance, love and care is considered useless, or held to be an intolerable burden, and is therefore rejected in one way or another. A person who, because of illness, handicap or, more simply, just by existing compromises the well-being or lifestyle of those who are more favoured tends to be looked upon as an enemy to be resisted or eliminated."[10]

The problem today is not just that we forget or ignore our responsibilities to the weakest and most vulnerable people in society. That has always happened. Throughout history there have been countless children who neglect their elderly parents, parents who abandon their children, and people who don't take care of a sick or dying relative. But such failures in responsibility often were looked down upon and discouraged in society. What's new today is that our culture makes it easy to rationalize our selfishness in these weighty matters.

[10]John Paul II, *Evangelium Vitae*, March 25, 1995, no. 12.

Remains of Temple of Venus & Roma, Rome

It sometimes even encourages us to shrink from our responsibility to love those who need our love the most.

This is seen most tragically with the way we treat unborn human life. In the case of an unborn child, Saint John Paul II said no one more absolutely innocent and more in need of our love and care could be imagined. "He or she is *weak*, defenceless even to the point of lacking that minimal form of defence consisting in the poignant power of a newborn baby's cries and tears." Moreover, "The unborn child is totally entrusted to the protection and care of the woman carrying him or her in the womb."[11] Such a person calls us to greater love and service, not less. Though some try to argue that a baby in the womb is not a person, a new life begins at the moment of conception—a life that is neither the mother's nor the father's. This being would not become human life if it is not so already. The program of what this living being will become is already established at this point of fertilization: "a

[11] Ibid., no. 58.

person, this individual person with his characteristic aspects already well determined".[12] Any human life should be protected and treated with dignity, but especially a baby in the womb, who is so completely dependent on another and is so totally innocent and defenseless.

Certainly, an unwanted pregnancy is a harrowing ordeal for a woman, who suddenly feels her world has been turned completely upside down. But the Church also knows that trying to run away from this trial through abortion can be emotionally, psychologically, and spiritually traumatic as well. This is why many Catholic priests, bishops, and organizations have reached out to women in this distressing situation and offered to provide financial, emotional, and medical help if they choose to keep their babies. The Church also has devoted personnel and financial resources to help women who have suffered through an abortion. Many women experience post-abortion trauma, and they need our care and attention as well. They need to know how much God loves them, as well as how much he wants to forgive them and give them a new start in life. Some may need counseling; all need to know God's loving mercy.

So we see that the Catholic Church doesn't just say abortion is wrong. She calls us to share in the responsibility, not just to protect the unborn, but also to assist women with unwanted pregnancies, so they can carry their babies to term, and to help the many women have suffered through abortion.

The New Commandment

The night before he died, at the Last Supper, Jesus did something astonishing with his twelve apostles. He rose from the

---

[12] Ibid., no. 60.

table, poured water into a basin, and began to wash his disciples' feet.

Washing feet was the kind of task a slave would perform for his master. Yet, this is what Jesus, the Lord of the universe, did for his disciples (see Jn 13:1–20). The divine Son of God humbled himself, taking on the role of a slave, to show how much he loves and serves his people. In doing so, he called his followers to do the same for others. In fact, Jesus was showing us that serving others is a key characteristic of what it means to be a true disciple. He said, "A new commandment I give to you, that you love one another; even as I have loved you, that you also love one another. By this all men will know that you are my disciples" (Jn 13:34–35).

When we truly encounter Christ's love, it changes us. It changes our hearts. It changes our priorities: how we spend our time, how we spend our money, how we treat others, what we view as most important in life. In the process, we become more compassionate and desire to imitate Christ, humbly and sacrificially serving those around us. Instead of always grasping for our own pleasure, comfort, and gain, we find ourselves setting aside our own interests and going out of ourselves to "wash the feet of others". Rather than living with the attitude of indifference that says, "Am I my brother's keeper?" we assume more responsibility for our brethren in the human family.

This is the mark of a true disciple: the Holy Spirit gradually transforming his heart and reordering his life. True love of God will always lead to greater love of neighbor. If we experience God's gentleness and love day-to-day amid our own trials and weaknesses, if we truly encounter his mercy and grace amid our own struggles and sins, we cannot help but share the love we've experienced with others. Indeed, the more profoundly we encounter God's love in our own lives, the more his love will shine through us. It's only by surrendering ever more to this love of God within us—by saying yes to the Holy Spirit's promptings to give more and not to take, to love and not to use, to care for the weak and not to view them as a burden—that we will find our fulfillment in a life lived, not for self, but for Christ.

Chapter Sixteen

Prayer

The Encounter of God's Thirst with Ours

If you've ever felt that you're not that good at prayer, that you're distracted and restless, or that you're not even sure how to pray, you are in good company. Many of the great saints have struggled in prayer at various points in their lives. The great apostle Saint Paul himself once admitted, "[W]e do not know how to pray as we ought" (Rom 8:26).

Part of the reason we feel so inadequate may be that we view prayer as a performance. Prayer is often thought of simply as a spiritual activity good Christians are to carry out: We say our prayers. We go to Mass. We recite the Our Father, the Hail Mary, or the Glory Be. We read the Scriptures, talk to God, and listen to him. Prayer is something we are supposed to do for God. The performance is on our end, so we better do it very well. If we view prayer in this way, it's no wonder we struggle with it, give up, or don't bother at all.

But when the fourteenth-century Saint Catherine of Siena wrote about prayer, she focused more on God's role—God's desire for us. God loves us so much that, when he created us, he placed a longing for him in our hearts. He created us with infinite desires that only he could fulfill. And the God who ardently wants to be united with us is constantly appealing

The Woman at the Well, Augustine Institute Chapel, Denver

to those deepest desires, inviting us to turn more to him,
drawing us to seek him who alone can fulfill us. In prayer,
God in his love for us draws out our desire for him. According to Saint Catherine, this is what prayer is all about: "It is
the desire of God which draws to itself the desire that is
in the depths of the soul, in such a way that together they
make one thing."[1]

The *Catechism of the Catholic Church* makes a similar point
when alluding to the Gospel story of Jesus encountering the
Samaritan woman at the well.[2]

The story would have been shocking to the Jews in
Jesus' day, for the Samaritans were considered sinners who

[1] St. Catherine of Siena, *St. Catherine of Siena: Passion for Truth—Compassion
for Humanity*, ed. Mary O'Driscoll (Hyde Park, N.Y.: New City Press, 1993),
p. 22.
[2] See *CCC* 2560; Jn 4:1–42.

broke away from God's covenant people. And this particular Samaritan woman whom Jesus meets would have been viewed with even greater suspicion. She had been living an immoral life, having had five different husbands and currently living with another man. Many in first-century Judaism would wonder, "Why would Jesus spend time with a woman like this?"

Yet, Jesus doesn't just welcome this woman. He actually seeks her out, as if he has some pressing need to be with her. He leaves Judea, travels to Samaria, enters her world, and meets her in her village at the well. Jesus' first words to her are not "Repent!" or "Why don't you get your act together?" Nor does Jesus begin the conversation telling her how important he is for her as the Savior or how much she needs his truth, his mercy, his salvation. Rather, Jesus, the divine Son of God, does the most unexpected thing. He expresses *his need* for something *from her*. He says to her, "Give me a drink" (Jn 4:7). It's as if Jesus travels all the way to Samaria just to tell this woman about this urgent need, his thirst.

The *Catechism* uses this Gospel story as an analogy for our relationship with God in prayer. We are like the Samaritan woman, and it is as if Jesus is standing before us today, saying, "Give me a drink." But Jesus is thirsty for something much more than water. He thirsts for us. He thirsts for our love, our attention, our hearts. And one of the key ways we encounter Christ's thirst is in prayer. "It is he who first seeks us and asks us for a drink. Jesus thirsts; his asking arises from the depths of God's desire for us. Whether we realize it or not, prayer is the encounter of God's thirst with ours. God thirsts that we may thirst for him" (*CCC* 2560). Even the desire that we have to pray, we should realize, is actually prompted by God's desire for a relationship with us.

Knowing that God takes the initiative in prayer, that he thirsts for us, is moving. The God of the universe longs for our love! It's also comforting, for it takes a bit of the pressure off in prayer. I can move forward with prayer knowing it's not all about me and how well I perform. God wants this loving relationship even more than I do. My main job is to give him the space to work in my life, to cooperate with him, and allow him to draw out ever more from my heart my desire for him. As the *Catechism* explains, many quickly become discouraged in prayer "because they do not know that prayer comes also from the Holy Spirit and not from themselves alone" (*CCC* 2726).

The Heart

Knowing that prayer does not come from ourselves alone is a crucial point. There are many forms and expressions of prayer. There are also many times to pray, places to pray, and styles of praying. But the Catholic Church emphasizes that, at its core, prayer is "a vital and personal relationship with the living and true God" (*CCC* 2558). And this relationship with God in prayer is lived in the heart. In fact, the Bible mentions hundreds of times the human heart as the key place where this relationship with God is lived.

But what do we mean by "the heart"? In Scripture, the heart is the center of all my thoughts, attentions, and affections. The *Catechism* describes the heart as that "hidden center" or "dwelling-place where I am, where I live" (*CCC* 2563). In prayer, God wants to meet me there in my heart, not in my performance. He wants to draw out my desire for him in my heart. This is more central in prayer than how well I recite certain words, perform certain actions, or reflect on certain sacred texts. Certainly, all these and other pious practices are important tools God uses to reach our hearts,

Guiding Star Pilgrimages, LLC

Crucifix, Missionaries of Charity Chapel, Denver

and we should give the best of ourselves to them. But in the end, they are just tools. The crucial thing to keep in mind is that Jesus thirsts for our love, and prayer is a "response of love to the thirst of the only Son of God" (*CCC* 2561). How will we respond to that thirst? Living more in tune with those holy longings deep in our hearts is at the center of the drama of prayer.

Indeed, Saint Catherine of Siena taught that the greatest thing we can offer God is our "infinitely desirous love".[3] Pious practices, devotions, good works, and penances should be *expressions* of our love for God, but they in themselves are not the goal. They are means, not ends. God once told

[3] St. Catherine of Siena, *The Dialogue* (New York: Paulist Press, 1980), 42–43.

Saint Catherine, "I want works of penance and other bodily practices undertaken as means, not as your chief goal. By making them your chief goal you would be giving me a finite thing—like a word that comes out of the mouth and then ceases to exist—unless indeed that word comes out of the soul's love. I mean that finite works—which I have likened to words—must be joined with loving charity."[4] The *Catechism* similarly explains that the practices of prayer are of little value on their own: "If our heart is far from God, the words of prayer are in vain" (*CCC* 2562).

The Foundation of Humility

Humility is the foundation of all prayer. Whatever kind of prayer one may be offering—whether it's reciting a Rosary, praying with Scripture, or adoring Jesus in the Blessed Sacrament—the fundamental attitude we bring to those prayers is what's most important. And that attitude must be one of true humility.

Sometimes we can be tempted to approach prayer like a job interview, striving to do the right things, say the right words, give the right answers. We might admit our weaknesses, but even then, we quickly try to spin those into strengths: "I've sinned again. I'm weak. And I don't know how to pray well. But I'm working on it, God! I can't believe I did that.... I'll be better next time!"

But remember, God is not interested primarily in our performance. And he's not taken in by our polite speeches. More than anything else in prayer, he wants our hearts. Do we come to Jesus in prayer humbly as we really are, vulnerable

[4] Ibid.

before him? Do we approach him as beggars? Do we come to God confident that he loves us even amid our feeble attempts at prayer and Christian living? Most of all, are we convinced that it's precisely there—in our weaknesses, in our inability to pray well, in our struggles—that God wants to meet us? We often want to present ourselves well before our God and leave a good impression. Deep down, some of us wish we had our lives all together so that we didn't need his help and forgiveness as much. We wish we could bypass the need for his mercy. We also wish we knew how to pray well so that we could leave the chapel feeling good about ourselves. ("Wow, that was a good time in prayer. I'm getting really good at this!") But all this is a hidden form of pride. God is not interested in the masks we bring to prayer. And he is not waiting up in heaven for us to get our act together and climb up to him. He stoops down to us and wants to encounter the real person with all his real weaknesses, sins, fears, and dysfunctions. This is why the first step of prayer is humility. As Saint Thérèse of Lisieux once said to her sister Celine, "You wish to scale a mountain and the good God wants to make you descend; He is waiting for you low down in the fertile valley of humility."[5]

How to Pray

Think of prayer as a conversation with a close friend—someone who knows you very well and loves you. As with any relationship, it's important to have time in conversation for the relationship to grow. And the more important the

[5] St. Thérèse of Lisieux, *Counsels and Reminiscences*, http://www.ccel.org /ccel/therese/autobio.xxi.html.

relationship, the deeper and more frequent that conversation should be. That's why Christians should take some time every day for prayer—not just to say some prayers, but for intimate conversation with the Lord, a personal encounter with our God.

But how does one pray? Here are four simple things any ordinary Christian can do in their conversation with God. These points can be summed up with the acronym "ACTS": *a*doration, *c*onfession, *t*hanksgiving, and *s*upplication.

The first thing we can do in prayer is *adoration*. This is the basic human response to God's gift of himself to us. We who are mere creatures acknowledge God as Creator. In response to God's goodness and love, we adore him—we tell him we love him and bless him in return.

A second aspect of prayer is *confession*. Here, we refer not to the sacrament of confession, but to the daily practice of admitting our sins before God. As in any relationship, it's important to tell God we're sorry for the ways we have hurt the relationship, through our sins and failures to love. Taking time each day to consider what we've done wrong and what good we've failed to do helps us to express true sorrow for the ways we've fallen short in our relationship with God and neighbor. In this prayer, God meets us with his mercy, ready to forgive and to strengthen our relationship with him.

A third form of prayer is *thanksgiving*. This form of prayer is one we forget. We always ask God for things, but do we take time to thank him for all he has done for us—giving us life, dying for our sins, filling us with his Spirit? We should always express gratitude to God for his blessings, whether it be the people in our lives, the ways he provides for us, the ways he helps us in our need, and how he supports us through our sufferings. Most of all, we thank God for the spiritual blessings he bestows on us through his work of sal-vation and the life of faith.

Finally, *supplication* is simply presenting our needs before our heavenly Father. Supplication can take on two forms. On one hand, we should always pray for others' needs. We can pray for the poor, the sick, and the suffering. We can pray for peace and justice in the world. We can pray for specific friends and family members in their particular needs for God's help. These kinds of supplications are known as "intercessory prayer". On the other hand, we should also pray for our own needs and intentions, whether it be asking God for help in our job, wisdom in how to approach a parenting issue, guidance in a decision, grace to overcome a certain sin, or comfort in time of sorrow. God wants us to come to him with our needs, and this is called "prayer of petition".

These four basic forms of prayer—ACTS—are found throughout Scripture and the Christian tradition. They are expressions known as *vocal prayer*. We may speak to God aloud in a group, saying, "Thank you, God, for all your bless-ings!" Or we may whisper certain words on our own: "I love you, God", or "Jesus, help me." Or we may simply speak to God in our hearts: "Lord, I'm so sorry I did that. Please forgive me." Whether spoken aloud or silently in our hearts, vocal prayer uses words of praise, thanksgiving, sorrow, and supplication to feed our conversation with God.

Meditation and Contemplation

Another important form of prayer is *meditation*. In this prayer, "the mind seeks to understand the why and how of the Christian life, in order to adhere and respond to what the Lord is asking" (*CCC* 2705). It typically involves reflecting

From the *Symbolon* series

Church of the Holy Sepulcher, interior

on spiritual books such as the Scriptures, the writings of the saints, or other good spiritual classics such as *The Imitation of Christ* or *Introduction to the Devout Life*, or more contemporary works such as *My Daily Bread* or the reflections in *Magnificat*. These writings invite us to ponder more who God is, various aspects of the Christian life, and how we can imitate Jesus more. By prayerfully reflecting on these texts, we can talk to God about them and ask the Lord how certain points might apply to our life. In our meditation, we may find our hearts stirring to thank God for something or to praise him for his goodness. We might notice how an insight sheds light on a certain situation, problem, or discernment we've been facing. Meditation might also inspire conversion of heart. We may realize a certain sin in our lives that we didn't notice before and desire to tell God we're sorry. In this way, our meditation sometimes feeds our vocal prayers of adoration, confession, thanksgiving, and supplication. It also may lead to a deeper knowledge of the love of Christ and union with him in a form of prayer known as *contemplation*, which is simply a still, loving attentiveness to God himself—a love that surpasses what any words may express. Saint Teresa of Avila described contemplative prayer as "a close sharing between friends ... taking time frequently to be alone with him who we know loves us."[6]

But whatever words we speak or forms of prayer we use, we must remember how in prayer we are responding to God's desire for us. He wants our hearts. So vocal prayer, meditation, and contemplation are not ends in themselves. They should be expressions of the heart's loving response to the God who so loves us. And the fundamental disposition of humility helps create the interior space for God to draw out our desire for him in these various expressions of prayer.

The Battle for Prayer

The life of prayer is not easy. We will face many trials along the way, including the challenge of making time to pray, distractions, dryness, and the feeling that our prayers are not being heard.

One challenge is *the problem of time*. Many Christians might admit prayer is important, but they claim they don't have time to pray. Pressures at work, busyness of family life, and even participating in important activities in the Church are given as excuses for why they don't set aside some quiet time—fifteen, twenty, or thirty minutes each day—for intimate conversation with the Lord. "How could I possibly do that? I don't have time!"

That's an interesting statement: "I don't have time." In reality, we all have time. The question is, what are we doing

[6] St. Teresa of Avila, *The Book of Her Life*, 8, 5, in *The Collected Works of St. Teresa of Avila*, trans. K. Kavanaugh, OCD, and O. Rodriguez, OCD (Washington, DC: Institute of Carmelite Studies, 1976), I, 67.

with our time? What are our priorities in life: Success? Financial gain? Sports? Entertainment? A thrilling social life? We make time for the things we value most. We take time out for the activities we consider vital. People usually don't die of hunger because they don't take time to eat. But do we view prayer as an absolutely vital endeavor? Pope Francis once compared prayer to breathing. Just as we need to take in oxygen to survive, so we need to take in what he calls "the deep breath of prayer" if we want to sustain the Christian life.[7] When we don't take time for prayer, however, it may be an indication, not so much of our busyness, but of where our hearts really are. "For where your treasure is, there will your heart be also" (Mt 6:21; Lk 12:34). A life without regular prayer may be a sign that we don't value God as much as we should. It may even point to a certain pride. If we were humbly convinced of our nothingness, of how much we really need God, of how little we could do without him, we would be rushing to the chapel regularly, stopping in the middle of our day to tell him we love him, to ask for his guidance, and to beg for his help. We would make the time for prayer in our daily lives. But someone who claims to be too busy for prayer subtly thinks he can actually get by in life on his own—in his job, family, moral life, and Christian living. Jesus wants to meet you each day in prayer. He is thirsting for you at the well. Will you take time to meet him in prayer?

A second challenge in prayer is *distraction*. We may take time to talk to God and meditate on the Scriptures, but our minds wander. We're trying to reflect on Jesus in the Gospel

[7] Francis, Apostolic Exhortation *Evangelii Gaudium*, November 24, 2013, no. 262.

Pilgrims praying at Santo Spiritu in Sassia Church, Rome

reading, but we find ourselves thinking about what we're going to eat for breakfast, a problem at work, or something someone said to us yesterday ("What did she *mean* by that?"). Distractions like this happen all the time to good Christians at Mass, in the chapel, or at home in prayer. What should we do?

Realize that a distraction reveals what we're attached to: pleasure, our career, our reputation, a desire to be liked. These aren't necessarily bad things when pursued in the proper way, but in prayer, they keep us from what's most important. The *Catechism* offers good advice on how to handle distracting thoughts. Rather than let the distraction agitate us, we can actually use the distraction as a moment to grow in humility and turn our hearts back to God. We can simply admit to the Lord our attachment to this project, this sin, or this anxiety over a certain trial in our life, and then tell God how he is more important than whatever has entered our minds. "All that is necessary is to turn back to our heart: for a distraction reveals to us what we are attached to, and this humble awareness before the Lord should awaken our preferential love for him and lead us resolutely to offer him our heart to be purified" (*CCC* 2729).

A third common struggle is *dryness in prayer*. For those who sincerely want to pray and give the best of themselves to God in prayer, dryness, especially prolonged dryness, is one of the greatest crosses they will face in their spiritual lives. Sometimes in prayer, God blesses us with delight and consolation. But in other moments or even seasons, the soul feels as if it is not close to God. The person gets no "feedback" from God in prayer and has "no taste for thoughts, memories, and feelings, even spiritual ones" (*CCC* 2731). Prayer itself seems pointless. Why does this happen?

God sometimes withdraws the feelings of his closeness because of some sin or rejection of God. Our faith lacks roots or we have turned away from God in a certain way, and we need conversion. But sometimes, God removes the feelings of his closeness simply to test our hearts, to test if we are coming to prayer for the good insights and good feelings we experience, or for him alone. In these moments of dryness, what will we do? Will we turn away from prayer because it's too hard, not as interesting, or not as pleasing anymore? Or will we prove our love for our Lord by persevering in prayer even though we don't feel as if we are getting much out of it? For the souls who remain faithful in prayer, God draws out their desire for him even more, for now their love is being purified. They are coming to prayer, not for what God showers onto the soul, but for God himself—not for the gifts, but for the Giver of the gifts.

A fourth struggle people have in prayer is *complaining of not being heard*. "I keep praying and praying, but God doesn't seem to be answering my prayer!" This is a real cross for many good Christians. The *Catechism*'s teaching on this topic sheds light on this. First, we should consider whether we treat God as our heavenly Father who knows what's best for us and wants our happiness even more than we do. Or do we treat him like Santa Claus or a spiritual genie who is there to answer all our requests?

> We ought to be astonished by this fact: when we praise God or give him thanks ... we are not particularly concerned whether or not our prayer is acceptable to him. On the other hand, we demand to see the results of our petitions. What is the image of God that motivates our prayer: an instrument to be used? or the Father of our Lord Jesus Christ? (*CCC* 2735)

The reality is that God *always* hears our prayers and answers them. He may not answer them in the ways we want him to, but as our heavenly Father, he knows infinitely more than we do what is truly best for us. We should, therefore, approach prayer with great humility, acknowledging that we may not always know what is best. Even if our prayer is for something good—the healing of a loved one, the conversion of a family member, reconciliation with a friend—we must trust that God hears our prayers but that his timetables and his ways are not our own. Our love and good intention in that prayer is caught up into God's larger plan, but his plan may involve greater goods—for us, for the person we're praying for, and for the world as a whole—greater goods that we cannot see with our limited perspective. If I continuously pray, for example, to overcome a certain sin, God might allow me to continue to struggle with that weakness— not because he doesn't love me or doesn't want to help me, but because there are other areas he wants to address first. I think the main problem is X, but God is calling me to grow in humility, patience, or compassion on others. We may not always get what we initially were looking for in prayer, but we will always get what we need.

This is why we should bring our petitions before God in a humble way, like the leper in the Gospel account who approached Jesus, saying, "Lord, if you will, you can make me clean" (Mt 8:2). Notice how the leper didn't tell Jesus what to do. He expressed his desire and his need, but he entrusted the matter entirely to Christ's will. We should do the same. We should accompany our petitions with that same spirit of detachment and humility, saying, "Lord, if it be your will ..."

In fact, in the process of pouring our hearts to God in prayer, something amazing often happens: our desires themselves can become softened or transformed. We may notice ourselves being a little less attached, a little more open to other possibilities, a little more trusting that God's plan in a certain matter is truly better than our own. When this happens, our hearts are surrendering more to God, and our desires are being shaped more by his will than our own. This is part of the great work God wishes to accomplish in us through prayer. As Saint Augustine said, "God wills that our desires should be exercised in prayer, that we may be able to receive what he is prepared to give."[8]

Indeed, God always has something wonderful in store for us, even if it's not what we were expecting or hoping for. No matter what trials, sufferings, or crosses we face, Christians must have the hope-filled confidence that there is some good that God can bring from it in our lives and in the world. Maybe that good thing is not something we will understand for some time. It might also be something interior: a greater

---

[8] Augustine, *Ep.* 130, 8, 17: *PL* 33, 500.

surrender, a greater trust, an invitation to walk more by faith and not by sight. In the processes of prayer, however, we are being prepared to welcome whatever God wishes to give us. As one early Christian said, "Do not be troubled if you do not immediately receive from God what you ask him; for he desires to do something even greater for you, while you cling to him in prayer."[9]

[9] Evagrius Ponticus, *De oration* 34: *PG* 79, 1179.

CONCLUSION

Faith and Discipleship

"I *believe* in one God ..." One simple word at the beginning of the Creed—"believe"—challenges us to ask ourselves a crucial personal question: "What is the foundation for my life? In what do I place my trust?"

Belief has two main aspects (see *CCC* 150). On one hand, it is something intellectual: the mind assents to all that God has revealed. But belief also entails a "personal adherence to God", an entrusting of oneself to God (ibid.). And this is typically the more challenging part. It's one thing to believe that God exists. It's another thing to entrust your life to him. Yet, allowing the faith to shape one's entire life is at the very heart of what it means to be a faithful Christian.

One biblical word for belief expresses this point particularly well. The word in Hebrew is *'aman*, from which the word "amen" is derived. The word can mean to trust, to entrust one's self, or to take one's stand on something else. In this light, we can see that faith is about "taking a stand trustfully on the ground of the word of God".[1]

The opening line from the Creed, "I believe in one God ... ", invites us, therefore, to do more than express an

[1] Joseph Ratzinger, *Introduction to Christianity* (San Francisco: Ignatius Press, 1990), 39.

intellectual conviction that God exists. It calls us to entrust ever more of ourselves to him. It challenges us to consider honestly where we seek our happiness: Is God truly the number one priority in my life? Or do I seek security and fulfillment in other things—my career, possessions, being liked, approval from others? Do I allow God to be my foundation, entrusting my dreams, plans, hopes, and fears to him? Or do I seek to control everything for myself—believing God exists, but holding back my heart and refusing to commit a certain part of my life to him?

Throughout this book, we have journeyed through the "big picture" of the faith. We've seen how, at its heart, the Catholic faith is the story of God's love. It's about a God who created us out of love with a plan for our happiness. It's about a God who, even in the face of our sin, still loved us so much he sent his Son, Jesus Christ, to die for us, to forgive us and reconcile us to himself. It's about a God who loved us so much he gave us his Church to guide us and the sacraments to fill us with his life and strengthen us on our way.

Indeed, the God who is love revealed himself to us. Like a bride unveiling herself to her bridegroom, God unveils himself to us so that we might respond to him in love. And our God is constantly inviting us to draw closer to him and take the next step in this love story.

How will you respond? Hopefully, in this walk through the Catholic faith, you have encountered insights from the tradition that stirred you to thank God, to praise him, and to give more of yourself to him in love. Perhaps you felt moved to read Scripture, go to confession, or go to Mass more often. Or maybe you sensed God wanting you to make a certain change in the way you are living. Perhaps you felt drawn to forgive someone who hurt you or serve someone in need. Or maybe you just think you need to spend more time with God in prayer each day. Whatever God may be putting on your heart and mind, ask him to guide you and to give you the grace to respond generously. And remember, Jesus calls us not simply to believe certain things *about* him. He calls us to believe *in* him—to entrust ourselves to him and to live as lifelong disciples. May you always move forward on your journey of faith with Jesus and the Church, so that you can say with Saint Paul and all the saints in heaven, "I have fought the good fight. I have finished the race. I have kept the faith" (2 Tim 4:6).

INDEX

abortion, 11, 256
Adam and Eve, 52–53, *53*, 54,
   55
adelphoi (brothers), 150
adoration, in prayer, 144, 203,
   266, 268
afterlife, 157–69
   heaven in, 156, 158–59, 160,
      161
   hell in, 156, 159–60, 161
   judgment in, 155, 157–58,
      168–69
   love in, 167–68
   prayers for deceased, 167–68
   purgatory in, 156, 160–61,
      162–64, 165–68, 165n10
   spiritual purification in,
      164–67
agape, 248, 249, 251, 253
Alexamenos Graffiti, 83, *85*
anchor inscriptions, in
   catacombs, 157, *158*
angels, 49–51
Annunciation, 146
Annunciation, Basilica of the
   (Nazareth), *14*
anointing of sick, 184
answers to prayers, 272–75
apostles. *See also specific apostles*
   authority of, 43, 58–59, 76–77,
      125, 130, 179, 220–22

Holy Spirit and, 41–42, 41n11,
   58–59, 100–102, 176
apostolic succession, 125, 126,
   129, 130–33
Ark of the Covenant, 145
Ascension, 97, 99
Assumption, of Mary, 144,
   151–52
Athanasius, Saint, 104
Augustine Institute Chapel
   (Denver), *260*
Augustine of Hippo, Saint, 22,
   23–24, 29–30, 98, 128, 180,
   274

baptism
   in ancient Rome, 170–72, 175
   common beliefs regarding, 125
   Holy Spirit at, 59, 102, 103
   of Jesus Christ, 71–73, 102
   physical elements of, 173, 175
   ritual words in, 173
   sacramental signs in, 180
   symbolism in, 170, 171–72,
      175, 183
   trinitarian faith exemplified
      in, 22
Baptism of Christ (Maratta), *23*
baptismal fonts, 170, 171
baptistries, 170, *171*, *174*
Barron, Robert, 20, 95–96

279

Love Unveiled: The Catholic Faith Explained

A *Symbolon* Resource

This book is based on the acclaimed film series *Symbolon: The Catholic Faith Explained*, led by Dr Edward Sri. The *Symbolon* series provides readers with the dynamic "big picture" of the Catholic faith and covers the four main dimensions of Catholic life:

- what Catholics believe (the Creed)
- what they celebrate (the Sacraments)
- how they live (the moral life)
- how they communicate with God (prayer)

Symbolon: The Catholic Faith Explained features outstanding presentations by Greg and Julie Alexander, Jim Beckman, Johnnette S. Benkovic, Patrick Coffin, Lisa Cotter, Mandy Cox, Jason Evert, Crystalina Evert, Martha Fernandez-Sardina, Tim Gray, Magdalena Gutierrez, Mary Healy, Deborah Holiday, Sean Innerst, Curtis Martin, Julianne Miles, Fr. Leo Patalinghug, Lucas Pollice, Scott Powell, Jonathan Reyes, Scott Sollom, Chris Stefanick, Jared Staudt, Michel Therrien, Teresa Tomeo, and Katie (Peterson) Warner. *Symbolon: The Catholic Faith Explained* was produced by the Augustine Institute and is available from Ignatius Press and through Formed.org.